For Afro-Dominican chef Nelson German, drinks and food are about connection—whether it's sharing stories over cocktails with family at home or gathering with friends under the warm, buzzy lights of his restaurants. In *Caribbean Cocktails,* you'll find simple yet inventive recipes for beverages and bites that bring the vibrant drinking and food culture of the Afro-Latino diaspora straight to your home bar and kitchen, spotlighting the ingredients that make the culinary history so unique.

Six sections exploring distinct flavor profiles—warm & sweet; floral, fruity & herbal; sour & bitter; spicy; and salty & smoky—offer a rich selection of recipes, with contributions from well-known bartenders and chefs throughout. Whip up twists on classics like Sorel Negroni and Captain's Final Word, modern creations like Cabana Rum Punch and Dominican Date Sour, and enticing sweet and savory bites like Coconut Rum–Caramelized Sweet Plantains and Dungeness Crab–Stuffed Piquillo Peppers. And for folks who love the flavors but want less of the booze, there are plenty of low-ABV and alcohol-free variations.

With the unique, historically based, flavorful recipes in *Caribbean Cocktails,* you'll soon be entertaining impressively at home.

Caribbean Cocktails

Brugal
MAMA JUANA
"MI Dón"

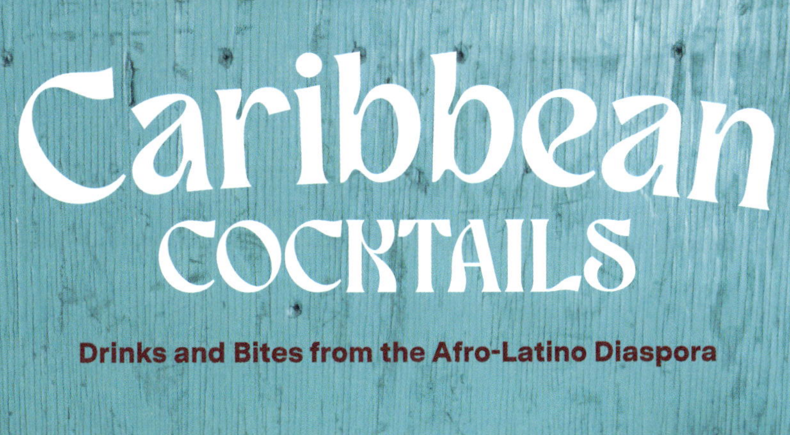

Caribbean COCKTAILS

Drinks and Bites from the Afro-Latino Diaspora

Nelson German
and Andréa Lawson Gray

Photographs by Eduardo Gonzalez (LemonAd Media)
Illustrations by Fanesha Fabre

TEN SPEED PRESS
California | New York

To my wonderful son, Mason Carlos German—
You are my greatest joy and my daily inspiration. May you always walk in your truth, carry your heritage with pride, and know that your roots are powerful, beautiful, and unbreakable.

And to my Afro-Latino community—
This is for us. For our flavors, our rhythms, our resilience, and our brilliance. May this book be a celebration of who we are, where we come from, and where we're going. Siempre con orgullo.

CONTENTS

THE FIRST POUR

First Fridays in Oakland, California, where I own and operate my two restaurants, are busy and buzzy. Back when First Fridays started in 2011, they were a great way to support Oakland's then-budding (now blossoming) restaurant scene. For AlaMar, my first restaurant, First Friday was the busiest night of the month. It wasn't a great night to be short-staffed, much less at the bar. But that's exactly what happened in 2018.

As a small business owner, you jump in where you're needed, so I jumped behind the bar. Thing is though—I had no experience as a mixologist or when it came to interacting with our customers. I had always been in the kitchen, cooking my heart out. So there I was, feeling something between cool and nervous, adrenaline flowing for sure. The first cocktail I made was a twist on a daiquiri, tapping into what I had seen other bartenders do. Of course, I used rum—the most Dominican of liquors and a very familiar ingredient to me.

Before long, I realized riffing on cocktails felt kinda like cooking. To be honest, AlaMar was a success, and with everything running relatively smoothly, a kind of ennui had set in. Jumping behind the bar was a spur-of-the-moment choice at the time, but it gave me a much-needed spark, a new challenge. Creating cocktails felt familiar, but also different, fresh, and exciting.

Being face-to-face with the guests was also new, but to my surprise, the showmanship and storytelling that come part and parcel with bartending came naturally to me. It transported me back to hot New York summer evenings in The Heights (Washington Heights) where I grew up, to block parties and *chismeando* (gossiping) on the stoop. In a way, that first night behind the bar at AlaMar set me on the path that would eventually put me in front of the camera on *Top Chef*, and it laid the groundwork for other TV and social appearances—and for this book.

When I first started bartending, I was eager to learn, and eager to show my respect for those who had been behind the bar for years. Immersing myself in the craft deepened my appreciation for its artistry. I found inspiration from talking to colleagues and neighbors, learning their perspectives and techniques. It was especially exciting to engage with other people of color in the industry, hearing their stories and building a supportive network. I am honored to have several of these talented individuals contributing recipes to this book as "guest bartenders." This sense of community has been integral in shaping my journey.

Creating cocktails is really an art form, a craft—just like making food. I started to look for excuses to put myself behind the bar, honing my craft until it became my new passion. Soon, word spread, and friends started showing up to support me, hang out, and share stories. I was having fun—fun with friends, fun with customers who would become friends, and fun using my knowledge of flavors and ingredients in a new way.

What started as a spontaneous decision slowly turned into something real. And now, years later, it's come full circle: I have a bar of my own in Oakland where those same kinds of connections are still being made, one cocktail at a time. It's also where I get to bring in the lessons I learned from my uncles—the ones who taught me how to pour rum with respect, how to make Mamajuana, and that every bottle comes with a story. Those early conversations, shared over music, laughter, and family meals, are the root of everything I create behind the bar at Sobre Mesa today.

My Culinary Soul

Wherever people of African origin found themselves because of the Atlantic slave trade, they created food. That food is now foundational to the Afro-Latino communal identity not only in the Dominican Republic, where my mother was born, but throughout the diaspora.

This book is an exploration of my Afro-Latino roots, of my never-ending personal journey of discovery, shared through a culinary lens. Some of the recipes in this book are my mother's dishes; others are my interpretations of my Dominican grandmother's beloved recipes. Some are creations all my own, still informed by everything that came before me.

Coming to realize, truly understand, and embrace my dual identity was a game-changer. Life in my Dominican NYC neighborhood of Washington Heights revolved around community. Everybody knew each other by block; we shared food and swapped stories. The neighborhood smelled and sounded Dominican, with aromas wafting from the open windows as everyone's moms made fried plantains, *gallina guisada* (stewed chicken), and *moro* (Dominican beans and rice), all punctuated by the sounds of merengue and bachata music.

No one talked about our African roots, much less acknowledged them. We were Latinos. We were not from Africa. Only it turns out, we were. In fact, my memories of my childhood—those smells wafting down the block, the food I ate growing up—are what would eventually lead me to explore my African heritage, and later express and share it through my cooking and bartending.

I remember the day a Black family dining at my first restaurant, AlaMar, asked about the Black owner they had heard about. A staff member responded, "This isn't a Black-owned restaurant; this is a Dominican-owned restaurant." That hit me hard. My family are Black Dominican Americans—part of the Spanish-speaking African diaspora. I realized I hadn't done enough to highlight my Blackness or its role in shaping who I am. And it made me think about how much the African continent has influenced the culinary world.

I saw that what I was doing with drinks wasn't just creative—it was cultural reclamation.

That realization deepened when I appeared on *Top Chef,* where a challenge centered on African cuisine brought everything into focus. It reminded me that the flavors I grew up with—plantains, braised meats, rich spice blends—weren't just Dominican; they were African, too.

The food world has gradually started to make space for these connections and embrace a wider array of ingredients and culinary history—but the cocktail world is still catching up. Too often, the contributions of the African diaspora flavors—ingredients like sorrel, kola nut, tamarind, Grains of Paradise—are left out of the conversation entirely. The stories behind these ingredients, the ancestral knowledge, the migration paths they've taken—they're all right there, just waiting to be explored. I had already opened Sobre Mesa less than a year before filming *Top Chef,* but that experience shifted something in me. I saw that what I was doing with drinks wasn't just creative—it was cultural reclamation. It was time to bring the full weight of our flavors and stories into the cocktail glass.

Initially, my bar leaned more into Latino flavors, but after my experience on *Top Chef*, I knew I had to dive even deeper. The cocktail world was under-representing and under-utilizing the spices, ingredients, and stories tied to the African diaspora. I wanted to change that. I wanted to honor this vast history and culture not just through food but also through drinks, blending them together to tell a richer story.

You can see it in the *Top Chef* episode—the joy, the recognition, and the memories sparked by that meal. Eating that food, experiencing those flavors, and recognizing the connections gave me a renewed sense of purpose. It was the moment I truly understood the depth of my culinary identity and the path I wanted to take.

These moments didn't just make me reflect on my own identity—they reminded me of how gatherings are central to Dominican culture, and how much we rely on food *and* drink to bring people together. I experienced it every day growing up. Whether it was a wedding, a baptism, or a Sunday with family, we weren't just sharing a meal—we were building community. My aunties, my grandmother, my tíos—all of them knew how to set a table that felt like home. And while the plates were full of Dominican staples, there was always something to sip on, too. There were homemade juices made from whatever fruit might be growing in someone's yard—passion fruit, guava, sour orange, tamarind, mango. And tucked somewhere behind the bottles, there was always Mamajuana (see page 40)—dark, spiced, a little mysterious. Every family had their own mix and method for it.

The women taught me how to cook—how to build flavor, feed a crowd, and show love through food. The men taught me about rum.

I used to think my Dominican aunties—and my grandmother—had taught me everything there was to know about our food and traditions. The summers I spent as a child in the Dominican Republic were a kind of finishing school, filling in the gaps in a way only hands-on experience can. The women taught me how to cook—how to build flavor, feed a crowd, and show love through food. The men taught me about rum. And when I was old enough, my uncles added to that education by showing me how to make Mamajuana—a traditional drink that, while originally created by women for medicinal and fertility purposes, has long been passed down through the men of the family. They walked me through the ritual like it was a rite of passage—selecting the bark blend, layering the rum and wine, watching it infuse over time. It wasn't just about the drink—it was about tradition, memory, and learning by doing.

So, imagine my surprise at discovering so many new and amazing things about the DR during the process of creating *Caribbean Cocktails*! I learned about small immigrant populations, like the descendants of formerly enslaved African Americans who made their way to the Samaná Peninsula who, as it turns out, were the originators of one of my very favorite childhood snacks, Yaniqueques (page 57). I learned about ingredients I hadn't ever associated with the Dominican Republic, like macadamia nuts,

Gracias Ancestros, page 74

which are now grown on the island and appear as an ingredient in this book (La Loma, page 33, and Dominican Coffee Cake with Guavaberry Caramel Sauce, page 110). And I heard origin stories that had been long hidden, even deliberately obscured, like the fact that the fermentation knowledge essential to the rum industry was likely influenced by the expertise of enslaved Africans, who brought their knowledge of fermentation to the Caribbean. Working on this book taught me there's still so much more to discover—about the ingredients, the stories behind the drinks, and the ways we celebrate who we are with what we pour into a glass.

The chapters that follow offer a deeper look at the Afro-Latino experience through flavor, tracing the people, places, and histories that have inspired the cocktails and small plates in this book. We begin with the cultural foundations of the Afro-Latino-Caribbean identity.

Who Are Afro-Latinos in the Caribbean & Beyond?

Afro-Latinos in the Caribbean—and across Latin America—are the descendants of African peoples brought to the region through the Transatlantic Slave Trade, whose identities have been shaped by a fusion of African, Indigenous, and European influences. While often grouped together, Afro-Latinos are culturally and historically diverse, with distinct traditions across countries like the Dominican Republic, Cuba, Puerto Rico, Colombia, Venezuela, and coastal Central America, as well as parts of Mexico and Peru.

In the Caribbean, African heritage is not a subtext—it is foundational. You see it in the rhythms of salsa and bomba, in the use of plantains and root vegetables, in spiritual practices, language, and, of course, in the food and drink. Afro-Caribbean traditions in Latin America often thrive in the margins—rural areas, fishing villages, barrios—and have been historically underrepresented in mainstream Latinx narratives. But these communities have been instrumental in shaping what we recognize today as Caribbean Latinidad.

To identify as Afro-Latino is to carry layered histories of survival and cultural creation. It's not only about ancestry. It's about lived experience, often tied to race, region, language, and class. This book doesn't attempt to define Afro-Latinidad as a monolith but instead highlights the flavors, stories, and spirits that emerge from this rich and ongoing conversation between heritage and homeland.

The Dominican Republic

The Dominican Republic (or the DR, as it is affectionately called) is the second-largest Caribbean island by area, bigger than the sum of all the other West Indian islands excluding Cuba. It also has the third-largest population, over eleven million as of 2023. Prior to colonization, *Quisqueya,* the Indigenous name for the island Columbus called Hispaniola, was home to the Taíno, an Arawak people who also inhabited most of Cuba, Jamaica, Puerto Rico, and the Bahamas.

Dominican cookery and cocktail culture represent a crossroads of Taíno, Spanish, and African foodways and drinking traditions—as do the people of the DR. This rich fusion is evident everywhere in today's Dominican Republic, where the people, the flavors, the music, and the art are an almost seamless blend of the ghosts from the island's past. Even Mamajuana—the spiced concoction often considered to be the country's national drink—is a reflection of that legacy. Its foundation in herbal infusions traces back to Taíno practices, later layered with rum, wine, and honey through colonization and cultural exchange.

Hospitality is king in the DR, and the capital city, Santo Domingo, has been honored as a "Culinary Capital of the Caribbean" by the Ibero-American Academy of Gastronomy—recognizing the significance of traditional Dominican recipes and fine dining as essential parts of the nation's culture. And that same spirit of creativity and celebration is reflected not just on the plate, but in the city's dynamic cocktail bars, lounges, and beachside spots, where local flavors and island influences are captured in every pour.

From island to island—and beyond—the rhythm changes, but the spirit in the glass remains bold, joyful, and undeniably ours.

It is a true honor—and the realization of a lifelong dream—to bring the Dominican Republic's Afro-Latino mixology—and a small taste of Dominican cuisine—to the fore. While many of the recipes in this book are rooted in my Dominican background, I also spent months researching other parts of the Caribbean, West Africa, Latin America, and beyond to ensure that the ingredients, stories, and techniques are thoughtfully represented. From island to island—and beyond—the rhythm changes, but the spirit in the glass remains bold, joyful, and undeniably ours.

Sorel Negroni, page 49

HOW TO USE THIS BOOK

The six chapters are organized around the flavor profiles of key ingredients in the drinks and bites: warm and sweet; floral, fruity, and herbal; sour and bitter; spicy; and smoky and salty. Any cocktail (or spirit-free mixed drink) in a given chapter pairs with the food recipes in that same chapter, so you have the freedom to experiment with your own combinations. For those who prefer more guidance, I've sprinkled pairing suggestions throughout. Aside from recipes, each chapter also includes an introduction that explores the cultural and historical background of the ingredients featured—why they matter, where they come from, and how they've shaped the Afro-Latino culinary landscape.

Given the wide range of rum styles and production methods—each of which affects flavor—I specify which type of rum to use for each cocktail. Occasionally, you'll see a general description, like "blended aged Caribbean rum"; in these cases, you're free to choose your preferred brand. If you're curious to learn more about rum styles, production, and history, you'll find a deep dive in Sipping Memories (page 28) at the start of Chapter One, Cálido, Tibio y Dulce.

Across all spirits, specific brands are named when they're core to the cocktail's flavor profile. Along the way, you'll encounter some rare and less-familiar bottles—embrace the discovery; it's all part of the adventure. Building a well-stocked bar may mean picking up a few new spirits, but your cocktail game will be better for it. Where flexibility allows, I've suggested a few favorite brands to help guide your selection.

Finally, nearly all cocktail recipes yield a single drink unless otherwise noted. With that said, many are also great to make in larger quantities. Called "batching," this technique lets you prep drinks (or components) ahead and store them in the fridge or freezer. It's a great way to save time, especially when you've got a few friends coming over. You'll find more on how to do that in Behind the Bar (page 19). Recipes that don't work well for batching are marked with the Not Batchable icon, as seen below.

You'll also notice that in the method sections, I use a little bit of mixologist shorthand to describe techniques—for example, "dry shake," "double strain," or "float gently over the back of a spoon." If you're new to these, don't worry! You can easily refer to the Behind the Bar section for a quick guide to what each term means and how to do it.

Icons to Guide You

To help you navigate the drinks in this book, I've included a few icons that offer quick insight into a cocktail's vibe or complexity:

Spirit-Free: These potions—or their variations—are fully nonalcoholic, crafted with the same intention, balance, and flavor-forward approach as their boozy counterparts, but they require a bit more finesse in the final steps. Because zero-proof drinks lack the structure, viscosity, and preservative qualities that alcohol provides, they're more vulnerable to dilution and flavor loss. To preserve their balance and boldness, chill your glassware and shaker ahead of time, and shake or stir gently and for less time than you would with full-proof cocktails. You can find a list of all spirit-free cocktails and variations on page 175.

Low-ABV: Cocktails in this category use low-alcohol ingredients like aperitifs, wines, or liqueurs to create nuanced drinks with less kick. Several cocktails include a low-ABV variation after the main recipe. You can find a list of all low-ABV cocktails and variations on page 175.

Not Batchable: Because many of the cocktails in this book are well-suited to advance batching, we've chosen to highlight only the few that *cannot* be batched. You'll see this icon next to recipes that are best made "à la minute" due to texture, separation, or ingredient stability. A list of ingredients that can't be batched is included later in this chapter. If a cocktail recipe does *not* have the "not suitable for batching" icon, it can be prepared ahead of time using the batching guidelines in Behind the Bar (page 19).

Large-Yield: This icon flags recipes or subrecipes that yield more than you'll need for a single drink—think of it as your cue to get creative with the leftovers.

Showstopper: These drinks stand out for their theatrical presentation, rare ingredients, or techniques that take a little more time—like coconut oil–washing Scotch (page 145) or making a house shrub.

A great cocktail is more than just spirits and mixers—it's the layers of detail that bring it to life. I've included a section toward the end of the book called From Scratch (page 155), with recipes for homemade syrups, infusions, and garnishes that are used in the cocktails. Some of these recipes—like Banana Syrup or Guajillo Chile Agave Syrup—are quick and easy. Others, like Corn Coconut Milk or Candied Yam Syrup, require a little more effort, but they'll reward you with deeper flavor and more nuance.

At the very end of the book, you'll also find an index of cocktails organized by alcohol type, including any specific brands called for in recipes. It's also a great way to find multiple cocktails (and bites) that use the same bottle—so if you pick up something special like Nixta or Sorel, you'll have plenty of ways to enjoy it again and again.

Whether you're just beginning your journey or you're already a seasoned mixologist, this book invites you to explore, experiment, and enjoy the art of building flavor. I'd love to hear from you as you travel through the Afro-Latino diaspora, whether from behind your bar or in your kitchen. What pairings did you love? Which cocktails were your favorites? What personal twists did you add? Drop me a message on Instagram @chefnel4 and let me know!

DAY RUM
SAFFRON
PASSION FRUIT LIQUEUR
BRUGAL
AÑEJO
MONTENEGRO
MAMA JUANA
"Mi Dôn"
DAY RUM
Sirop J.M
TEN TO ONE
CARIBBEAN DARK RUM
BOUKMAN
AMARGO
Chuncho

BEHIND THE BAR

This section is a quick-reference guide to the language, tools, and techniques of cocktail making. You may already have some of the bartender essentials listed here; others are worth adding if you're looking to elevate your setup—of course, all in the name of "research"!

Mixology Terms & Definitions

Batching: Most cocktails in *Caribbean Cocktails* can be "batched"—meaning you can make them ahead of time and store them in the fridge or freezer. This is a great option for parties, prep-ahead service, or anytime you want to simplify your flow behind the bar.

Cocktails that contain citrus juice can be fully batched and refrigerated for short-term storage, up to a day in advance. If you're prepping more than a day in advance, omit the citrus juice and add it fresh just before serving. Citrus juice loses its freshness fast—it can become flat, bitter, and can even cause the cocktail to separate if it sits for too long. You'll find a short Chef's Note at the end of recipes where this applies.

To batch a cocktail, follow these steps:

1. Combine all ingredients listed in the recipe, except citrus and garnishes.
2. To simulate the dilution that occurs during shaking, add 1 part cold water for every 4 parts cocktail, replicating the effect of melting ice.
3. Pour into a clean bottle or jar with a tight seal.
4. Label with the date, ingredients, and number of servings.
5. Store in the refrigerator for up to 5 days, or freeze for up to 2 months, depending on the ingredients.

To serve a batched cocktail, simply pour it into the appropriate glass—no shaking or stirring required.

However, not every cocktail holds up well over time. These drinks are marked with a Not Batchable icon (see page 16). Recipes that include the following ingredients should always be made to order.

- Egg whites, aquafaba, or cocktail foamer: These ingredients do not keep well, even in the fridge, and will lose their texture.
- Citrus juice: This will lose freshness and acidity.
- Dairy-based ingredients (e.g., cream, milk and plant-based "dairy" like coconut cream and nut milks): These can separate or develop off-flavors.
- Sparkling wine, Champagne, or beer: These will lose carbonation.

Cocktail foamers: Liquid alternatives to egg whites used for creating froth and texture in cocktails without changing the flavor. Add a few drops to your shaker, then dry shake (without ice), and then wet shake (with ice).

Dash: A common bar measurement that equals 1/32 ounce (about 1/8 teaspoon).

Double strain: Straining a cocktail through both the strainer built into the shaker and a fine-mesh strainer to remove pulp, ice shards, or other fine particles.

Dry shake: Shaking cocktail ingredients without ice to mix or create foam before shaking with ice (the "wet shake") to chill and dilute the drink.

Float: Pouring (or "floating") a lighter liquid over a denser one using the back of a spoon to gently layer it on top of the cocktail without mixing.

Neat: A spirit served plain, at room temperature, without ice, water, or mixers, usually in a rocks glass.

Saline solution: Saline solution appears in several cocktails throughout this book, typically added by the drop. It plays a subtle but crucial role in balancing flavor, especially in drinks that include citrus, bitter-edged ingredients, or tropical fruit. Unlike adding salt directly, which can be uneven or overly assertive, saline solution allows for precise control and a cleaner integration of salinity into the drink. I recommend a 10% saline solution: Add 10g of fine sea salt to 100g of room temperature water and stir until fully dissolved. Store at room temperature in a clean glass dropper bottle.

Shrub: A syrup made from fruit, sweetener, vinegar, and spices, and lightly fermented for a tangy, sweet-sour flavor. While often used in cocktails, shrubs like the Orange Shombo Shrub (page 118) and Watermelon Shrub (page 121) are equally delicious topped with sparkling water or used in dressings and marinades.

Simple syrup: A sugar syrup made by combining equal parts sugar and water over heat, often infused with other flavors. To make simple syrup,

Mark del Caribe, page 139

add equal parts sugar and water to a small saucepan over medium heat. Stir until the sugar fully dissolves, then bring to a gentle simmer. Reduce the heat to low and simmer gently for 5 minutes. Remove from the heat and cool completely before using. Store in an airtight container in the refrigerator for up to 2 weeks.

Spirit rinse: Swirling a small amount of spirit around the inside of a glass to coat it before discarding the excess. This adds subtle aroma and flavor to the cocktail.

Spirit spritz: Finely misting a spirit over a cocktail or glass to add a subtle aroma or flavor without altering the drink's balance. Typically done using an atomizer or spray bottle, a spirit spritz is often applied to the surface of a finished drink or inside the glass before pouring the cocktail. Common spirits used for spritzing include absinthe, citrus-infused spirits, and flavored liqueurs.

Splash: A common bar measurement that equals ⅕ ounce (about 1 teaspoon).

Top off: Adding a final ingredient, typically a liquid like soda, tonic, or sparkling wine, to fill the glass and complete the cocktail.

Wet shake: Shaking cocktail ingredients with ice to chill, mix, and dilute the drink.

Zero-Proof Bar Ingredients

Zero-proof spirits have come a long way. The best of them now deliver the structure, spice, brightness, and depth that were once only possible with alcohol. In the recipes throughout this book, we use them not as stand-ins, but as intentional building blocks. They're chosen for how well they capture the essence of rum, Tequila, whiskey, Mezcal, and more.

Each of the zero-proof spirits listed here appears in at least one drink in this collection. All are widely available online or from specialty retailers, and most are shelf-stable once opened. When used in the proportions specified, they hold their own in stirred, shaken, and even clarified formats—bringing full flavor without compromise.

Zero-Proof Spirit	Replaces	Used In	Use
Abstinence Cape Citrus	Mezcal (citrus-forward)	Lake Breeze (page 141)	1:1 substitution
Abstinence Cape Floral	Light or blended rum	La Lucia (page 46), Santa Rosa (page 36), Bon Swa (page 72)	1:1 or as specified
Abstinence Cape Malt	Rye or whiskey	Gingerbread Holiday Milk Punch (page 51), Moka on the Table (page 99)	1:1 substitution
Abstinence Cape Spice	Spiced rum, whiskey, or amaro	La Loma (page 33), Coconut Daiquiri (page 67), Chocolate de Maní (page 95), Cafecito de la Mesa (page 103), Spice Me Down (page 117), Tropical Noir (page 91)	1:1 or as specified
Abstinence Epilogue X	Cointreau or orange liqueur	Lake Breeze (page 141)	1:1 substitution
Lyre's Dark Cane Spirit	Dark rum	La Lucia (page 46)	Used in combo with other nonalcoholic ingredients
Ritual Zero Proof Tequila Alternative	Tequila	Last Conacado (page 101), Valdez Punch (page 69)	1:1 substitution
Ritual Zero Proof Whiskey Alternative	Whiskey or bourbon	Doña Rosa (page 105), La Cultura Old Fashioned, (page 93)	1:1 substitution

Bar Equipment

Barspoon: Used as a tool, a barspoon is a long-handled spoon designed for stirring cocktails. Its length allows it to reach the bottom of tall mixing glasses or shakers, and its twisted handle often aids in controlled stirring and layering liquids. Used as a measurement, it typically holds ⅛ ounce (3.7 mL), which is roughly 1 teaspoon. However, in cocktail recipes, it is often rounded up to ¼ ounce (7.5 mL) when measuring liquid ingredients.

Bartender's/Chef's torch: A compact but powerful tool used to produce a precise, high-heat flame for culinary applications, including igniting wood chips when smoking cocktails. While often associated with brûlée-style desserts, a chef's or bartender's torch is essential for incorporating smoke into cocktails using a smoke top or cloche. Used in La Cultura Old Fashioned (page 93) and Cafecito de la Mesa (page 103).

Jigger or shot glass: A jigger is a two-sided conical cup used to measure liquor for cocktails. The most common jigger is 1½ ounces on the larger side (also the volume of a shot glass) and ¾ ounce on the smaller side.

Cocktail shaker and/or strainer: A cocktail shaker mixes and chills drinks by shaking ingredients with ice. Some shakers have built-in strainers, so you can pour directly. If yours doesn't, or if you're using a mixing glass instead of shaking, you'll need a separate strainer (such as a Hawthorne strainer) to keep ice or solids out of the finished drink. A strainer alone is useful when stirring rather than shaking.

Fine-mesh cocktail strainer (or fine-mesh strainer): A small handheld strainer with fine wire mesh, used in addition to a shaker's built-in strainer or Hawthorne strainer to catch small particles like pulp, crumbs, or ice shards.

Mixing glass: A tall glass used with a barspoon for stirring cocktails. It gently mixes drinks without shaking, preserving their clarity and texture.

Muddler: A tool for crushing fruits, herbs, or sugar cubes to release their flavors into a drink.

Smoke tops and wood chips: Used to infuse cocktails with smoke, smoke tops sit over a glass rim and hold wood chips—typically oak, cherry, hickory, or applewood. When ignited with a torch, the chips produce smoke that funnels into the glass, perfuming the headspace. A handheld smoking gun offers more control, but smoke tops easily enhance aroma at the glass. Used in Mark del Caribe (page 139) and Over-the-Table Old Fashioned (page 146).

Glassware

Barrel mug: A ceramic or glass mug designed for tiki or tropical-style cocktails, typically 12 to 16 ounces, sometimes larger.

Collins glass: A tall, slender glass perfect for cocktails with soda or other mixers, like a Tom Collins, typically 10 to 14 ounces.

Coupe: A stemmed glass with a shallow, rounded bowl, ideal for classic and shaken cocktails, typically 5 to 7 ounces.

Double rocks glass: A larger version of the standard rocks glass, typically used for drinks served "on the rocks" (over ice) or cocktails that have multiple ingredients and require more space. The capacity usually ranges from 10 to 14 ounces.

Flute: A type of stemmed glassware designed primarily for serving sparkling wines, such as Champagne, prosecco, and Cava, typically 6 to 10 ounces. Its narrow shape helps retain carbonation and concentrate aromas.

Highball glass: A tall, straight-sided glass typically holding 8 to 12 ounces. It has a slightly wider diameter than a Collins glass, making it well-suited for spirit-and-mixer cocktails such as The Latinidad Is Libre (page 88) or Spice Me Down (page 117). The highball glass allows for a balanced ratio of ice to liquid, helping maintain the drink's chill while preventing rapid dilution.

Hurricane glass: A tall, curved glass commonly used for tropical and blended cocktails, typically 16 to 20 ounces.

Nick & Nora glass: A small, elegant glass used for spirit-forward or stirred cocktails, typically 5 to 6 ounces.

Rocks glass: A smaller glass for drinks served on the rocks, like old fashioneds or Negronis—typically 6 to 10 ounces.

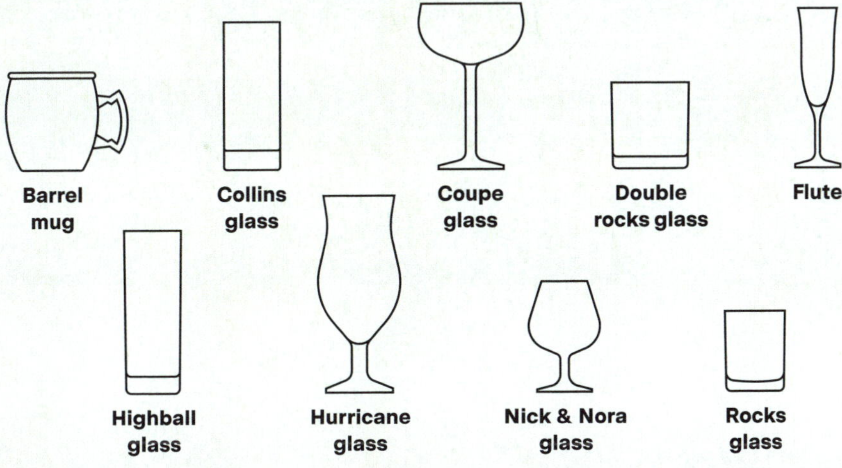

CÁLIDO, TIBIO Y DULCE

WARM & SWEET

COCKTAILS

33 **La Loma**
blended aged rum, macadamia nut milk, corn coconut milk, banana syrup, coffee liqueur, orgeat, nutmeg

35 **Candied Culture**
apple whiskey, Cognac, Cointreau, candied yam syrup, soursop

36 **Santa Rosa**
spiced rum, Sorel Liqueur, chocolate syrup, marshmallow syrup, Amarula, Old Man Guavaberry Rum Liqueur

39 **The Heights Mamajuana**
Dominican rum, red wine, honey, tree bark, warm herbs, spices

41 **To Die Dreaming**
Dominican rum, allspice dram, hibiscus syrup, orange juice, tangerine juice, orgeat syrup, Angostura bitters

44 **Chan Chan**
rhum agricole, yerba maté spiced honey, lime, banana syrup, egg white, calabash

45 **Chen Chen**
rhum agricole, Dominican rum, Nixta Licor de Elote, apricot, spiced wildflower honey, lime

46 **La Lucia**
Panamanian rum, Jamaican rum, Sorrel, cinnamon syrup, pineapple juice, lemon, ginger

49 **Sorel Negroni**
gin, Campari, sweet vermouth, Sorel Liqueur, orange

51 **Gingerbread Holiday Milk Punch**
whiskey, ginger liqueur, oloroso sherry, black tea, corn coconut milk, lemon, apple pie spice, vanilla

BITES

53 **Plantain Masa Arepas with Honey-Garlic Shrimp**

55 **Pollo Guisado Party Wings (Dominican-Style Braised Chicken Wings)**

56 **Plátanos al Ron (Coconut Rum–Caramelized Sweet Plantains)**

57 **Yaniqueques**

Sipping Memories

The warm and sweet flavors of rum—notes of caramel, molasses, and spice—make it an essential expression of the Caribbean's culinary traditions, aligning naturally with the culture and spice-forward dishes that define the region and the flavor profiles of this chapter.

For me as an Afro-Dominican, rum is so much more than a staple of the Dominican Republic—it is *corazón* (heart) and *tradición*. When I reached adulthood, my father, uncles, and grandfathers welcomed me to the next stage of life with rum and their life stories—a rite of passage I will always treasure and one I hope to share with my kids when the time comes. Rum is more than just delicious and versatile; it's personal, representing the stories, connections, and moments shared while sipping it, waiting for the food that brings us together. As a tradition and art form, rum has brought economic growth, jobs, celebration, and memories to my people, making it a true symbol of our culture.

The History of Rum in the Caribbean

Rum's origins trace back to the Caribbean in the seventeenth century, where it emerged as a byproduct of the booming sugar industry and quickly gained a reputation as a potent and transformative spirit. Early accounts refer to it as "kill-devil," a term steeped in colorful lore. Some suggest it earned this name because, as noted in *British Food in America*'s article "Rum, The Spirit of the Indies," "a man who imbibed it promptly became boisterous, reckless, and daring." Others believe it was so named for its purported ability to "[drive] the devil out" of enslaved people suffering from illness after exposure to cold nights. These stories reflect the potent and transformative reputation rum held from its earliest days.

Rum Production in the Caribbean

The rise of sugarcane cultivation across the Caribbean led directly to rum production. Without chattel slavery, there was no sugar—and since it's essentially a byproduct of sugar, the same can be said for rum. Molasses, a thick syrup left over from processing sugar, became the key ingredient in rum. Enslaved Africans in the Caribbean who were forced to work in sugarcane fields and processing mills played a central role in the development of rum, often adapting fermentation techniques from Africa, where sorghum beer had been made for millennia. By using these techniques, molasses could be transformed into a fermentable base for distillation. The process of making rum—fermenting molasses with water and yeast, followed by distillation to produce a high-alcohol spirit—has remained largely unchanged for centuries, a testament to the ingenuity and resilience of its beginnings.

Rum's production and consumption—and the culture surrounding it—were inseparable from the brutal realities of chattel slavery. The grueling labor on sugar plantations drastically shortened the lives of enslaved workers, many of whom survived only an average of seven years after arriving in the Americas, according to the National Museum of African American History and Culture. Even in death, their labor persisted in the rum trade, as barrels of rum were used as currency to purchase more enslaved people—thereby fueling the Transatlantic Slave Trade.

DISTILLERY JUSTICE

Historian and author Michael Twitty defines culinary justice as "the idea that oppressed peoples have the right to not only be recognized for their gastronomic contributions, but they have the right to their inherent value; to derive from them uplift and empowerment." His work laid much of the foundation for how we examine food, power, and identity—particularly in African diasporic cultures.

Inspired by this framework, we've coined the term "distillery justice" to describe the idea that rum's history—and future—must fully acknowledge the contributions of the enslaved and their descendants, whose labor and knowledge built the industry. The rum world is beginning to confront this legacy, reclaiming the spirit as a source of Caribbean pride and post-colonial cultural identity.

For too long, rum has been marketed in ways that erase its origins, presented as exotic, escapist, and disconnected from the people who cultivated and distilled it. But some producers today are working to change that narrative. Trinidadian entrepreneur Marc Farrell launched Ten to One Rum to challenge outdated stereotypes about Caribbean rum. Ian Burrell, co-founder of Equiano Rum (featured in Cabana Rum Punch, page 87), ties his brand directly to abolitionist history, naming it for Olaudah Equiano, a Nigerian-born freedman who fought to end slavery.

By centering labor, culture, and historical truth, these leaders—and many rum educators, historians, and distillers—are advancing the work of distillery justice: building a more honest and inclusive future for the spirit and the people behind it.

Overproof Rum: A Bold Legacy

The earliest rums were universally high-proof, with alcohol levels that often exceeded 75% alcohol by volume (ABV). This extraordinary potency made them suitable for storage, transport, and even use as currency in trade. Over time, as distillers refined their techniques, rums of varying proofs were developed to meet different tastes and uses. Today, overproof rum is typically defined as exceeding 60% ABV (40% ABV is standard). Overproof rums remain a cornerstone of Caribbean mixology, their bold flavors and intensity used—albeit in small amounts—to add depth to cocktails. They're both a tribute to rum's robust beginnings and a practical choice for modern bartenders seeking complexity in their drinks.

Types of Rum

Today, rum is crafted using various production techniques, resulting in distinct flavor profiles.

Agricole rum (rhum agricole): Made from fresh sugarcane juice, this French Caribbean rum has a grassy, vegetal profile with hints of fruit and earthiness.

Black strap rum: Dark, full-bodied rum made from blackstrap molasses, the deeply colored and intensely flavored byproduct of the final sugar refining stage.

Blended aged rum: A combination of rums aged for different lengths of time and often in different types of barrels. For example, rum aged five years in American oak might be blended with rum aged three years in charred oak to create a smooth profile with vanilla, caramel, and light smoke.

Double barrel–aged rum: Rum aged in one type of barrel, then transferred to another for added complexity. For instance, rum aged in heavily charred American oak could be moved to lightly toasted French oak, adding notes of spice and dried fruit.

Gold rum or amber rum: Versatile medium-bodied spirit aged in oak barrels, which gives it a warm golden hue and notes of vanilla, caramel, and mild spice. This category bridges the gap between light and dark rums, offering more depth than white rum without the heavy molasses flavors of dark rum.

Navy strength rum: Bold rum with 57% ABV.

Overproof rum: Rum exceeding 60% ABV. Once the standard, overproof rums are used sparingly in cocktails due to their potency and are now a specialized category, prized for their intensity.

Single barrel–aged rum: Rum bottled from a single cask, offering a pure expression of the barrel's unique influence.

Spiced rum: Rum infused with spices, herbs, and sometimes caramel or vanilla for added depth and sweetness. Typically made with gold or dark rum, it features flavors like cinnamon, clove, nutmeg, and allspice, with some varieties incorporating citrus or pepper. See page 158 for a homemade version.

White rum: Clear, light-bodied rum distilled from sugarcane byproducts, typically aged briefly in stainless steel or oak and charcoal-filtered for purity. With subtle notes of vanilla, citrus, and sugarcane, its mild flavor makes it a versatile base spirit, distinguishing it from richer, barrel-aged rums. Clairin is a traditional Haitian spirit distilled from sugarcane juice that falls under the category of unaged white rums. It is often recognized for its bold, grassy, and earthy character, with a flavor profile that reflects the natural fermentation and small-batch production methods used in its crafting.

The Warm & Sweet Flavor Family

This flavor family is built around ingredients that evoke warmth, comfort, and depth—cinnamon, nutmeg, clove, ginger, and other spices deeply rooted in Afro-Caribbean and Latin American cooking. These flavors don't just enhance rum—they mirror it.

- allspice (Jamaican pepper)
- cardamom
- cinnamon
- coconut
- cloves
- cumin
- ginger
- Grains of Paradise or Guinea grains
- mace
- nutmeg, calabash nutmeg a.k.a. ehuru

TO EACH ISLAND, ITS OWN

"If you want to know more about the type of rum from an island, all you need to do is get under the skin of its music, its food, and its general culture, and you can always draw a straight line to the kind of rum that's drunk there," says rum expert and Plantation Rum brand ambassador Paul McFadyen. That insight resonates deeply with me. In my travels throughout the Caribbean, I've tasted those differences firsthand—how each island's rum carries the rhythm of its people, its music, its history. Every place has its own pulse, and you can feel it in the glass—whether the rum is bold and funky, smooth and sweet, or spiced with the flavor of home. The culture shapes the spirit, just like the spirit helps define the culture.

Barbados rums are known for their easygoing balance, offering a flavor that's neither too heavy nor too light. Their smooth, versatile character makes them perfect for sipping or mixing. Jamaican rums, on the other hand, are bold and unapologetically rich, with a full-bodied intensity that stands out in any drink. Much like reggae and dancehall—the island's iconic music styles—Jamaican rums are vibrant, dynamic, and unabashedly bold, with notes of tropical fruits, warm spices, and molasses.

Cuba, the Dominican Republic, and Puerto Rico—all former Spanish colonies—lean toward sweeter, lighter styles of rum. Dominican rums are smooth and sweet, often with hints of vanilla, caramel, and dried fruit. Many are aged using the Spanish-originating *solera* method, where younger and older rums are blended in stages to create consistency and depth of flavor. The Dominican Republic alone has fifteen distilleries and produces 90 percent of the rum it consumes, reflecting the deep integration of rum into the country's culture and economy. Cuban rums are crisp and dry, with citrus and floral notes that make them ideal for cocktails like the classic mojito. Puerto Rican rums are light-bodied and versatile, featuring tropical flavors like coconut and vanilla—and they're the star ingredient in the world-famous piña colada.

In French-speaking islands like Haiti, Guadeloupe, and Martinique, rhum agricole takes the spotlight. Made from fresh sugarcane juice instead of molasses, it has a grassy, herbal flavor that's entirely its own.

The rums featured in this chapter—primarily gold, spiced, and blended aged rums—highlight the warm, sweet, and spiced profiles that echo the region's culinary traditions and flavor memory.

La Loma

While researching coffee production for this book (see pages 95–105 for coffee-forward cocktails), I stumbled upon an unexpected gem: macadamia nuts grown in the Dominican Republic. Though often associated with Polynesia, macadamias have carved out a place within the island's culinary traditions, thanks to a fascinating history of resilience and innovation.

After Hurricane David devastated 70 percent of the country's agriculture in 1979, the environmental group Plan Sierra introduced macadamia trees from Australia to help reforest the land and restore eroded soil. With shallow roots ideal for intercropping, macadamia trees provided shade for coffee plants and an additional income source for farmers. Today, small-scale farmers are integrating macadamia cultivation into traditional farming, improving both sustainability and livelihoods. Inspired by this story, I knew I had to incorporate macadamia nut milk into a cocktail. The result is a drink that honors the deep connection between coffee and macadamia farming while bringing a rich, nutty depth to the glass.

- 2 ounces blended aged rum
- ½ ounce macadamia nut milk
- ½ ounce Corn Coconut Milk (page 169), or more macadamia nut milk
- ½ ounce Banana Syrup (page 162)
- ½ ounce coffee liqueur
- ¼ ounce orgeat syrup
- Freshly grated nutmeg, for garnish
- Macadamia nuts, for garnish
- 1 Morir Soñando Popsicle (page 43), for garnish (optional)

In a shaker, combine the rum, both milks, Banana Syrup, coffee liqueur, and orgeat syrup with the ice cubes. Shake vigorously for 20 to 30 seconds, or until well chilled, then strain into a chilled hurricane glass filled with crushed ice. Garnish with freshly grated nutmeg, a few macadamia nuts, and the popsicles for a playful touch.

Spirit-Free La Loma: Pre-chill the shaker and glass to minimize dilution. Replace the rum with Abstinence Cape Spice, and the coffee liqueur with cold brew concentrate. Make sure your orgeat syrup is alcohol-free. Combine the ingredients as instructed in the main recipe. Add 4 or 5 ice cubes to the shaker and shake gently for 8 to 10 seconds, until the shaker is frosted on the outside and the drink is well chilled. Strain and serve as directed in the main recipe.

Chef's Note: To make a blended La Loma, skip the straining and put the entire contents of the shaker into a blender. Blend until smooth and serve immediately.

Pairing suggestion: Pollo Guisado Party Wings (page 55)

Glassware

Hurricane

Ice

4 or 5 cubes (for shaking) plus 1 cup crushed (for serving, unless making a blended cocktail)

Candied Culture

This cocktail combines the warmth of Cognac and apple whiskey with the sweet, earthy depth of homemade Candied Yam Syrup and a bright hint of tropical soursop. The result is a balanced drink that's both rich and refreshing. The drink is garnished with a candied yam.

Chef's Note: Yams were a vital crop brought from West Africa to the West Indies on slave ships, serving as sustenance for enslaved people. True yams, which require tropical climates, are not cultivated in the United States. Instead, what Americans call "yams" are sweet potatoes, a misnaming that originated with enslaved Africans in the southern U.S., who used the Senegalese word for yam—*nyami*—to describe sweet potatoes. This recipe uses American sweet potatoes (commonly labeled "yams" in U.S. markets), not true African yams.

- **½ ounce apple whiskey**
- **1½ ounces Cognac**
- **¼ ounce Cointreau (or good-quality triple sec of your choice)**
- **½ ounce Candied Yam Syrup (page 164)**
- **½ ounce soursop purée (see page 117) plus ¾ teaspoon water, mixed well**
- **Candied yam slice (page 155) or orange twist, for garnish**

In a shaker, combine the whiskey, Cognac, Cointreau, Candied Yam Syrup, and soursop mixture with cubed ice. Shake vigorously for about 10 seconds, or until the shaker is frosted on the outside and the drink is well chilled. Double strain the cocktail into a chilled coupe. To finish, garnish the drink with a slice of candied yam or an orange twist.

Low-ABV Candied Culture: Use 2 ounces Abstinence Cape Spice in place of the Cognac and apple whiskey. Swap the Cointreau for Aperitivo Cappelletti (17% ABV) or Pierre Ferrand Dry Curaçao (18% ABV), then follow the main recipe.

Chef's Note: Both versions of this drink can be batched and refrigerated for up to 3 days. Neither version is suitable for freezing.

Pairing suggestion: Plantain Masa Arepas with Honey-Garlic Shrimp (page 53) or Coconut Rum–Caramelized Sweet Plantains (page 56)

Special equipment	Glassware	Ice
Fine-mesh cocktail strainer	Chilled coupe	½ to ¾ cup cubed (for shaking)

Santa Rosa

I named this cocktail for Santa Rosa, the church I used to go to as a kid. It's where the community in Washington Heights came to gather, and where warmth, tradition, and a touch of sweetness always followed the service. After church, Dominican coffee, pastries, and *dulces* (sweets) were often served, including *deditos de novia* (bride's fingers), which are thin baked pastry rolls stuffed with guava jam. Inspired by those post-church moments, this cocktail layers rich, spiced flavors with guava's tropical brightness and a smooth, creamy finish.

Chef's Note: Old Man Guavaberry Liqueur remains available in the U.S., though in limited quantities—some specialty liquor stores (e.g., Beards Hill, Spirits Unlimited), regional chains, and online platforms (like Instacart and store locators) currently carry stock. Ask your favorite local retailer or liquor store to check.

- **1½ ounces spiced rum (preferably Chairman's Reserve or Clove-Infused Spiced Rum, page 158)**
- **½ ounce Sorel Liqueur**
- **½ ounce dark chocolate syrup, such as Monin or Ghirardelli**
- **½ ounce toasted marshmallow syrup**
- **½ ounce Old Man Guavaberry Rum Liqueur**
- **½ ounce Amarula Cream Liqueur**
- **1 guava-dipped marshmallow, for garnish (optional, page 156) or Amarena or brandied cherry, for garnish (optional)**

In a shaker, combine the spiced rum, Sorel Liqueur, chocolate syrup, marshmallow syrup, guavaberry liqueur, and Amarula. Dry shake for about 15 seconds to combine. Add the ice to the shaker and shake again for 15 to 20 seconds, or until the shaker is frosted on the outside and the drink is well chilled. Strain into the chilled glass and garnish with a guava-dipped marshmallow for a playful touch.

Spirit-Free Santa Rosa: Chill the shaker and glass in advance to minimize dilution. Replace the rum with Abstinence Cape Floral and the Sorel Liqueur with Hibiscus Syrup (page 165). Replace the Amarula Cream Liqueur with ½ ounce coconut cream (or, for a closer match, a non-alcoholic cream liqueur such as Lyre's). In a shaker, combine these and the remaining nonalcoholic ingredients. Fill with ice and shake gently for 8 to 10 seconds, or until the shaker is frosted on the outside and the drink is well chilled. Strain into the prepared glass and garnish with the guava-dipped marshmallow or Amarena or brandied cherry.

Pairing suggestion: Yaniqueques (page 57)

Glassware

Chilled coupe or Nick & Nora

Ice

3 or 4 cubes (for shaking)

Yaniqueques, page 57

MAMA JUANA
“Mi Dón”
Resfriados - Sinucitis - Riñones - Dolor
Estomacal - Ulceras - Enfermedades
Venereas - Aumento Sexual.
Juan Francisco (Mi Don)
Receta de Tío Manuel
canelilla
anís estrella
palo de Brazil
palo Indio
bejuco de Indio
vino roja
miel

The Heights Mamajuana

Mamajuana (sometimes Mama Juana) is officially recognized as the national drink of the Dominican Republic. Its origins are debated—some trace it back to a medicinal elixir used by the indigenous Taíno, while others attribute it to healing practices brought over by enslaved Africans. Today, it's made by combining rum, red wine, and honey with tree bark, warm herbs, and spices. The resulting flavor is often compared to port or amaro.

I prepare my Mamajuana the way my uncle taught me, using star anise, allspice berries, hibiscus petals, cinnamon sticks, dried basil leaves, cloves, chicory root, eucalyptus leaves, and ginger root. A Mamajuana bottle can be refilled eight to ten times, or until the eponymous "mother" (sediment) starts forming at the bottom.

To prepare Mamajuana, you'll need a suitable bottle for infusing the rum with herbs and spices. You can use any clean, sealable glass bottle or jar, typically around 750 mL to 1 liter in size. Empty wine or liquor bottles work well for this purpose. When selecting a bottle for making Mamajuana, make sure it's made of glass and has a secure seal.

In the Dominican Republic, Mamajuana is traditionally served neat (on its own) or as a shot at room temperature. I prefer mine chilled and keep it in the refrigerator—a choice my grandma roundly rejects, rolling her eyes and saying, "¡No está bueno!" (That's not the way!)

Chef's Note: Premixed Mamajuana herbs are made by artisans in the Dominican Republic and are available for purchase online. The mixtures vary but often include *canelilla* (cinnamon bark), *clavo dulce* (clove), anis *estrella* (star anise), *palo de Brasil* (Brazil wood), *palo indio* (Indian wood), and *bejuco de indio* (Indian vine).

1 (2 to 3-ounce) package premixed Mamajuana herbs (see Chef's Note)

1 cup Dominican aged rum (such as Brugal or Barceló)

½ cup red wine (dry or semi-sweet)

¼ cup honey (adjust to taste)

Glassware

Shot glass

Prepare the herbs: Rinse the Mamajuana herbs thoroughly with water to remove any dust or residue and transfer to a clean bottle (see headnote). For additional cleaning, boil the herbs for 10 to 30 seconds in water, then strain through a fine-mesh sieve. Discard the water. Optional: To remove bitterness from the herbs, place the rinsed herbs in a clean glass jar or bottle. Fill the container with a neutral spirit—such as vodka—or water and let it sit at room temperature for 1 to 3 days in a cool, dark place. Strain through a fine-mesh strainer, discard the liquid, and return the herbs to the bottle.

CONTINUED

The Heights Mamajuana, continued

Make the Mamajuana: Add the rum, red wine, and honey to the bottle with the prepared herbs. Stir or shake gently to combine the ingredients. Seal the bottle tightly and allow it to sit for at least 2 weeks at room temperature to let the flavors meld. The longer it infuses, the more intense the flavor becomes.

To serve: Pour the Mamajuana into shot glasses and serve chilled or at room temperature. Refill the bottle with the same mixture of rum, wine, and honey to prepare additional batches. The herbs can be reused for several months but will gradually lose their potency. In future batches, adjust the proportions of rum, wine, and honey to suit your taste preferences.

MAMAJUANA

Mamajuana has been called a cure-all for just about everything—boosting your sex drive, kicking the flu, helping digestion and circulation, and even cleansing your blood, liver, and kidneys. As with so many cures our *abuelitas* (grandmothers) pass down to us, there's probably some truth to Mamajuana's curative reputation, thanks to the health benefits of the herbs and spices it's made with. As word spread of its magic, people in the Dominican Republic started making and selling their own versions, each claiming to "fix" something different depending on the ingredients.

Mamajuana's growing popularity didn't sit well with *El Jefe* (The Chief) General Rafael Leonidas Trujillo, who ruled the Dominican Republic as a dictator from 1930 until his assassination in 1961. Trujillo issued a decree that only certified medical professionals could produce and sell Mamajuana, effectively shutting down a vital source of income for many poorer Dominicans.

To Die Dreaming

More than just a drink, morir soñando is a Dominican staple—a creamy, citrus-kissed refreshment—sort of like an orange creamsicle in a glass—that evokes childhood memories and family gatherings. Found in homes and *colmados* (convenience stores) alike, this beloved beverage is as much a part of Dominican culture as merengue and dominoes. Its name, which translates to "to die dreaming," captures the indulgent, almost dreamy balance of rich dairy and bright citrus—two ingredients that, when mixed correctly, achieve a near-magical harmony.

This cocktail and its variations celebrate the morir soñando legacy in different forms: a creamy, spirit-forward cocktail with allspice dram for depth, a nonalcoholic smoothie (or slushie) showcasing its signature flavor, and popsicles for a frozen take.

Chef's Note: Unlike sweeter rums often associated with the region, Brugal Dominican rum's defining characteristic is its dry, refined profile, a result of its aging process exclusively in American oak barrels previously used for whiskey. This approach imparts flavors of vanilla, oak, and subtle spice while maintaining a clean, balanced character.

ANGOSTURA-INFUSED CREMA

- 5 dashes Angostura bitters
- 1 cup heavy cream

- 1¾ ounces Brugal Añejo Dominican rum
- ¼ ounce St. Elizabeth Allspice Dram
- ¼ ounce Hibiscus Syrup (page 165)
- ½ ounce frozen orange juice concentrate
- ¾ ounce tangerine juice
- ¼ ounce orgeat syrup
- 5 dashes Angostura bitters
- 1 tablespoon (½ ounce) Angostura-infused crema, for garnish
- Freshly grated nutmeg, for garnish

Make the Angostura-infused crema: In a blender, combine the Angostura bitters and heavy cream. Blend or pulse gently for about 30 seconds, until the mixture thickens and looks like soft serve—you don't want whipped cream. If not using immediately, store in the refrigerator in an airtight container for up to 3 days. Stir or whisk gently before serving to restore its texture.

Make the cocktail: Put the ice in a cocktail shaker, then add the rum, dram, Hibiscus Syrup, frozen orange juice concentrate, tangerine juice, orgeat, and bitters. Shake vigorously for up to 30 seconds, until the shaker is frosted on the outside and the drink is well chilled. Strain into the chilled glass. Top with the Angostura-infused crema and a light sprinkle of freshly grated nutmeg before serving.

CONTINUED

Special equipment	Glassware	Ice
Blender	Chilled highball	5 or 6 cubes (for shaking)

Spirit-Free Morir Soñando Smoothies or Popsicles

Makes 4 (9-ounce) smoothies, or 12 to 14 (3-ounce) popsicles

- **1 cup frozen orange juice concentrate, straight from the freezer**
- **1 cup evaporated milk**
- **½ cup sweetened condensed milk**
- **1 teaspoon apple pie spice, plus more for garnish (optional)**
- **2 cups ice (for smoothies or popsicles; omit if serving over crushed ice)**

To make a smoothie or chilled drink: Blend all ingredients until smooth. Blend with 2 cups of ice for a smoothie, or serve over crushed ice as a chilled drink. Garnish with more apple pie spice, if desired.

To make popsicles: Whisk the same smoothie mixture in a bowl until fully combined. Instead of pouring over ice, pour into popsicle molds and freeze at least 4 hours. To unmold, dip the popsicle mold briefly in hot water.

Pairing suggestion: Pollo Guisado Party Wings (page 55)

Special equipment

Blender; popsicle molds (for popsicles)

Glassware

Collins glass (for smoothie or drink)

Ice

2 cups cubed (for smoothie or popsicles) or crushed (for drink)

Chan Chan

Named in playful homage to the *Canchánchara,* the Chan Chan draws inspiration from the traditional Cuban drink—made with rum, lime, and honey—and nods to Mexico's rich sugarcane-distilling heritage. The country's tradition of working with sugarcane dates back to the early 1500s, when the Spanish introduced the crop.

Widely believed to have originated with the Mambises, Cuban independence fighters during the Ten Years' War (1868–1878) and the War of Independence (1895–1898), the Canchánchara was consumed before battle as a source of warmth, sustenance, and "liquid courage." Today, it continues to provide a warming boost—whether as a conversation starter among friends or a sip of history in every glass.

Chef's Note: A touch of calabash nutmeg (also called ehuru) is used here, not as a vessel, but as a flavoring agent. These dried seed pods, called "calabash" since they're hard and dry like gourds, are prized in Afro-Caribbean traditions. Calabash nutmeg imparts an earthy, subtly bitter note that adds to this cocktail's complexity.

1¼ ounces rhum agricole

¼ ounce Yerba Maté Spiced Honey (page 160)

¾ ounce limón criollo juice (or Key lime juice)

¼ ounce Banana Syrup (page 162)

1 egg white or 2 drops cocktail foamer (see page 20)

Freshly grated calabash nutmeg or nutmeg, for garnish

Banana chip or banana leaf, for garnish

If using egg white: In a shaker, combine the rhum agricole, Yerba Maté Spiced Honey, lime juice, Banana Syrup, and egg white. Dry shake vigorously for 20 seconds to mix thoroughly, until smooth. Then add the ice and wet shake for 7 seconds, until well chilled.

If using cocktail foamer: Wet shake all of the ingredients (with ice) for 20 seconds. Strain out the liquid, discard the ice, and return the liquid to the empty shaker (no ice). Dry shake for 7 seconds.

For both methods, double strain into a chilled coupe. Garnish with freshly grated calabash nutmeg, a banana chip, or banana leaf.

Chef's Note: The base for this cocktail can be batched without the egg white (or foamer) and stored in the freezer for several months. Store in a freezer-safe glass bottle with a tight seal, such as a flip-top or corked bottle. Add the egg white or foamer and calabash nutmeg when preparing individual servings.

Pairing suggestion: Dominican Chorizo "Kipe" Bites (page 79)

Glassware

Chilled coupe

Ice

½ cup cubed (for shaking)

Chen Chen

This recipe evokes the flavors of chenchén, a traditional Dominican cracked corn pilaf. The star of the show here is Nixta Licor de Elote, a Mexican corn liqueur that calls to mind atole, a traditional Latin American masa-based beverage that's often served hot. Its sweet, creamy profile has notes of toasted corn, vanilla, caramel, and lime.

- **1 apricot, cut into wedges (or ½ ounce apricot preserves)**
- **¾ ounce fresh lime juice**
- **½ ounce spiced Nigerian wildflower honey (or local wildflower honey)**
- **1 ounce rhum agricole**
- **1 ounce Brugal Añejo Dominican rum (or Flor de Cana 4 or Ron Abuelo 7)**
- **½ ounce Nixta Licor de Elote**
- **2 drops saline solution (see page 20)**
- **1 corn husk, for garnish, optional**
- **Fresh apricot wedge or honeycomb, for garnish**

In a shaker, muddle the apricot with the lime juice and honey to release its juices and create a flavorful base. Add both rums, the Nixta, and the saline solution, then add the cubed ice. Shake vigorously for 15 seconds to chill and combine. Double strain into the chilled coupe. Optionally, drape a strip of corn husk across the rim of the glass or shape it into a small twist and rest it on the side of the glass. Garnish with an apricot wedge or a piece of honeycomb.

Chef's Note: This drink can be batched and refrigerated up to 3 days in advance. Do not freeze.

Pairing suggestion: Plantain Masa Arepas with Honey-Garlic Shrimp (page 53)

Special equipment

Muddler or long-handled spoon, fine-mesh cocktail strainer

Glassware

Chilled coupe

Ice

½ cup cubed (for shaking)

La Lucia FROM ERNESTO ANTONIO GUILLETTE

This cocktail springs from the Afro-Panamanian heritage of Ernesto Antonio Guillette, affectionately called "Tito." Born in the Canal Zone to Panamanian parents, he spent summers immersed in his homeland's vibrant culture. Memories of harvesting mangoes, soursop, and sorrel from his grandmother's backyard shape his craft as a mixologist. Family traditions, like pairing spiced sorrel with sweet buns and ham at holidays, form the foundation for this drink. La Lucia—named after his late grandmother—is a personal tribute. She cooked with him, shared stories of her childhood, and taught him how to make sorrel—the recipe at this drink's heart. La Lucia honors Afro-Panamanian culture, reflecting Tito's journey and the traditions that inspire him.

Chef's Note: Heady with lush notes of vanilla, oak, and spice, Panamanian Ron Abuelo 12-year rum plays soft to Smith & Cross Jamaican rum's bold, brash funk, highlighting the difference in rums by terroir. Start this recipe at least 24 hours and up to 3 days in advance to allow the cinnamon to infuse the rum.

3 to 4 slices fresh ginger

1 ounce Ron Abuelo 12 (or another column still–aged Latin-style rum, such as Flor de Cana 12 or El Dorado 12)

¾ ounce Smith & Cross Jamaican rum

½ ounce fresh lemon juice

1 ounce homemade Sorrel (recipe follows) or hibiscus tea

¼ ounce pineapple juice

¼ ounce cinnamon syrup (or Spiced Honey Syrup, page 162)

Dehydrated lemon wheel (see page 155) or candied ginger, for garnish

Freshly grated nutmeg, for garnish

Place the ginger in a cocktail shaker and crush gently with a muddler. Add both rums, the lemon juice, hibiscus tea, pineapple juice, and cinnamon syrup (or Spiced Honey Syrup). Fill the shaker with ice cubes and shake vigorously for about 15 seconds. Double strain into a hurricane glass filled with crushed ice. Garnish with a dehydrated lemon wheel or candied ginger and grate nutmeg over the top before serving.

Spirit-Free La Lucia: Chill the shaker and glass in advance to avoid dilution. Replace the rums with 1½ ounces Abstinence Cape Floral and ½ ounce Lyre's Dark Cane Spirit rum alternative. Proceed with the rest of the recipe as written, shaking gently for 8 to 10 seconds. Garnish as above.

Chef's Note: Both versions of this drink can be batched and refrigerated for up to 3 days. Batch all ingredients except the lemon juice; add the lemon juice just before serving to preserve its brightness. Do not freeze.

Special equipment	Glassware	Ice
Muddler, fine-mesh cocktail strainer	Hurricane or rocks	3 or 4 large cubes (for shaking) plus ¾ cup crushed (for serving)

Sorrel (Spiced Hibiscus Tea)

Makes about 1 quart

4 cups water

½ cup dried hibiscus flowers (or 3 hibiscus tea bags)

2 cinnamon sticks

5 whole cloves

1-inch piece fresh ginger, peeled and sliced

½ cup sugar (or more to taste)

In a medium saucepan, combine the water, hibiscus, cinnamon sticks, cloves, and ginger. Bring to a simmer over medium heat. Cover, reduce the heat to low, and simmer for 10 minutes. Remove from the heat and let steep, still covered, for 10 minutes.

Strain the mixture through a fine-mesh strainer into a clean container, discarding the solids. While the liquid is still hot, add the sugar and stir until dissolved. Let cool completely, then refrigerate until ready to use. Sorrel will keep for up to 1 week in the refrigerator.

Special equipment

Large fine-mesh strainer

SOREL

The roselle hibiscus flower, known as "sorrel" throughout the Caribbean, is prized for its tangy, fruity flavor and striking red color. Food historian Michael Twitty describes it as "Black joy and Black survival and Black culture . . . all bound up in one cup of hibiscus." Made into a beverage, it takes in the name "Sorel." Traditionally served cold at holidays, it can also be enjoyed warm as a spiced tea. Globally, hibiscus is celebrated in many forms: as "bissap" in Senegal, "Jamaica" in Mexico, and "karkadeh" in Egypt. In the Dominican Republic, the plant is called "Sangre de Cristo" (Blood of Christ), while the beverage made from it is also known as "sorrel."

Sorel Negroni

The Negroni, one of the most iconic Italian cocktails, traces its origins to early twentieth-century Florence, where Count Camillo Negroni requested a stronger variation of his usual Americano cocktail—replacing soda water with gin (see Chef's Note). The result, a perfectly orchestrated mix of bitter, sweet, and herbal flavors, cemented its place in cocktail history. The Sorel Negroni (photograph on page 14) brings a bold twist to the classic, introducing Sorel Liqueur, a hibiscus-spiced aperitif with warm hints of clove, cinnamon, and nutmeg. This island-inspired re-do enhances the Negroni's bittersweet profile, adding depth and a vibrant, aromatic complexity while honoring its original spirit.

Chef's Note: Not to be confused with the coffee drink, the Americano cocktail is a classic Italian aperitivo made with equal parts Campari and sweet vermouth, topped with soda water. It's lighter and more effervescent than the Negroni, which famously swaps soda for gin.

1 ounce gin (London dry or botanical gin)

1 ounce Campari

½ ounce sweet vermouth

½ ounce Sorel Liqueur

1 orange peel, for garnish

1 dried hibiscus flower, for garnish (optional)

Fill a rocks glass with one large ice cube and set aside. In a mixing glass, combine the gin, Campari, sweet vermouth, and Sorel Liqueur with the cubed ice. Stir well for 20 to 30 seconds, until well chilled. Using a cocktail strainer, strain the mixture over the large ice cube in the glass. Express the orange peel over the drink, rubbing it around the rim before dropping it into the drink as a garnish. For an extra Caribbean touch, add a hibiscus petal.

Chef's Note: This drink can be batched and refrigerated for up to 3 days. Avoid freezing to preserve the structure of its fortified wine component (the vermouth).

Glassware

Rocks

Ice

1 large cube (for serving)
plus 1 cup cubed (for stirring)

Gingerbread Holiday Milk Punch

Makes 6 (6-ounce) servings

A double dose of ginger, from crumbled cookies and liqueur, adds spark to the rich, nutty depth of Amontillado sherry and whiskey, the partnership made smooth and soothing against a creamy backdrop. This cocktail layers ginger with the rich, nutty depth of Amontillado sherry and whiskey, balanced by the smooth texture of milk punch. Demerara syrup adds extra warmth, its subtle caramel and toffee notes bolstering the drink's velvety richness. Named after the Demerara district in British Guyana, this minimally processed cane sugar adds complexity while keeping its festive spirit front and center.

Chef's Note: For a dairy-free punch, substitute the whole milk with additional Corn Coconut Milk (page 169), and swap the heavy cream with unsweetened full-fat coconut cream.

- 2 cinnamon sticks
- 7 star anise pods
- 8 gingerbread cookies
- 9 ounces whiskey
- 3 ounces The King's Ginger Liqueur
- 2 orange wheels
- 3 ounces oloroso sherry (or cream sherry)
- 2 black tea bags
- 3 ounces Demerara Syrup (see page 165)
- ¾ cup Corn Coconut Milk (page 169)
- ¾ cup whole milk (see Chef's Note)
- 1 ounce fresh lemon juice
- ¾ cup heavy cream
- 1½ teaspoons apple pie spice (or 1 teaspoon pumpkin spice)
- 3 dashes vanilla extract
- 6 candied yam slices (page 155), for garnish
- Freshly grated nutmeg, for garnish

In separate batches, toast the cinnamon, star anise, and cookies in a dry skillet over medium-low heat. Toast for 1 to 2 minutes each, or just until fragrant; don't walk away: They quickly go from toasty to burnt. Set aside to cool. Reserve 6 star anise for garnish; crush 2 cookies and set aside the other 6 for garnish.

In a large jar or container, combine the whiskey, The King's Ginger Liqueur, orange wheels, sherry, tea bags, cinnamon sticks, one of the star anise pods, the crushed cookies, and Demerara Syrup. Stir in the Corn Coconut Milk, milk, lemon juice, heavy cream, apple pie spice, and vanilla. Refrigerate the mixture for at least 3 hours or up to 24 hours to allow the flavors to meld.

Strain the chilled mixture through a large fine-mesh strainer lined with a coffee filter into a wide-mouthed container. This will take time—but allow the punch to filter slowly. Once strained, serve the punch in a rocks glass over a large ice cube. Garnish each portion with a star anise pod, gingerbread cookie, candied yam slice, and freshly grated nutmeg. Enjoy immediately.

Spirit-Free Gingerbread Holiday Milk Punch: Use 9 ounces Abstinence Cape Malt in place of the whiskey and ½ ounce ginger syrup in place of the King's Ginger Liqueur; then follow the original recipe for serving and garnishes.

Special equipment	Glassware	Ice
Fine-mesh strainer, coffee filter	Rocks	1 large cube per glass (for serving)

Plantain Masa Arepas with Honey-Garlic Shrimp

Makes 24 (1-ounce) arepas, or 8 servings

Dominican arepas trace back to the foodways of the Taíno, Indigenous peoples who inhabited present-day Dominican Republic. Unlike South American versions, which are typically savory, griddled, and split for fillings, the true Dominican arepa is a sweet, pan-baked cornmeal cake, sliced like bread and often served for holidays. Here, I reimagine the arepa as a savory, bite-size base for honey-garlic shrimp—a fusion of Dominican flavor and South American form. Ripe plantains in the dough nod to the cake's original sweetness, creating a dish that blends memory, texture, and flavor.

Chef's Note: Different brands of masa harina absorb water differently; adjust the amount of water as needed if not using the Masienda brand. Shaping masa takes practice. Be patient if you're unfamiliar with the technique—you'll improve over time.

PLANTAIN MASA AREPAS

- ½ ripe plantain, peeled and chopped
- 2½ cups (300g) masa harina (preferably Masienda brand)
- 2¼ teaspoons kosher salt
- 1½ cups warm water, plus more as needed
- Vegetable oil, as needed

CHILE-LIME AIOLI

- 1 cup mayonnaise
- Zest and juice of ¼ large lime
- ½ teaspoon sriracha
- ⅛ teaspoon cayenne pepper
- Pinch of kosher salt

PICKLED CABBAGE

- ¼ cup apple cider vinegar
- 1 tablespoon honey
- Zest and juice of 1 orange
- Zest and juice of 1 lime
- ⅛ teaspoon ground black pepper
- 1 cup shredded cabbage
- 2 tablespoons chopped cilantro

HONEY-GARLIC SHRIMP

- Vegetable oil, as needed
- ¼ cup chopped garlic
- 1 pound medium shrimp (30 to 40), peeled and deveined
- 1 tablespoon Dominican sazón (preferably Loisa brand)
- 2 teaspoons kosher salt
- 1 teaspoon cayenne pepper
- 1 teaspoon black pepper
- 2 tablespoons honey

Special equipment

Food processor

Prepare the plantain masa arepas: Bring 1 quart of water to a boil in a small saucepan over high heat. Add the plantain and cook until fully tender and soft, 2 to 5 minutes; drain well. Transfer the plantain to a food processor and purée until smooth, then set aside to cool.

CONTINUED

In a large bowl, combine the masa harina and salt and mix thoroughly. Slowly pour in ¾ cup of the warm water, kneading with your hands until the mixture forms a cohesive dough. Incorporate the plantain purée, then gradually add the remaining ¾ cup warm water, continuing to knead until the dough is smooth and the ingredients are evenly combined. If the dough feels too dry, add water as needed until it reaches the ideal consistency. Divide the dough into 24 equally sized portions, roll into balls, and cover with a damp kitchen towel to prevent them from drying out.

Make the aioli: In a small bowl, whisk together the mayonnaise, lime zest, lime juice, sriracha, cayenne pepper, and salt until smooth. Cover and refrigerate.

Make the pickled cabbage: In a medium bowl, combine the apple cider vinegar, honey, orange zest and juice, lime zest and juice, and black pepper. Stir until the honey dissolves completely, then add the cabbage and toss until fully coated. Fold in the cilantro and let marinate in the refrigerator for at least 15 minutes before serving.

Prepare the shrimp: Set a large skillet over medium-high heat and add enough vegetable oil to coat the surface. Add the garlic and shrimp, sautéing for 1 to 2 minutes, until the shrimp turn opaque on each side and are partially cooked. Sprinkle in the sazón, salt, cayenne pepper, and black pepper, stirring to combine and evenly coat the shrimp. Add the honey and continue cooking for 3 to 4 minutes, until the shrimp are fully cooked and glazed. Remove from the heat and set aside.

Cook the arepas: Flatten each masa ball into a disk about 1½ inches in diameter and ¼ inch thick. Heat a comal or nonstick skillet over high heat, with just enough vegetable oil to lightly coat the surface. Working in batches, cook the arepas for 20 to 30 seconds per side, until the surface is dry and lightly set with just a hint of browning. Remove from the heat and gently pinch the edges of each arepa upward to form a shallow rim, like a mini tart shell. (If they're too hot to handle, use a small spoon to shape the edges.) Add more vegetable oil to the skillet and set it over medium-high heat. Return the pinched arepas to the skillet, frying for about 1 minute per side, until golden and crispy. Transfer to a paper towel–lined plate.

Assemble: Fill each arepa with a tablespoon of shrimp, top with pickled cabbage, and drizzle with chile-lime aioli. Serve immediately.

To store arepas: Cooked arepas should be cooled completely before storing. To refrigerate, place in an airtight container or resealable plastic bag and store for up to 3 days. To freeze, arrange arepas in a single layer on a baking sheet and freeze until solid, then transfer to a freezer-safe bag or container and keep frozen for up to 3 months. Reheat from frozen by toasting or pan-frying until warmed through.

To store aioli and cabbage: Refrigerate chile-lime aioli for up to 5 days, and pickled cabbage for up to 1 week, both in airtight containers. Stir the aioli before using.

Pairing suggestion: Candied Culture (page 35) or Chan Chan (page 44)

Pollo Guisado Party Wings (Dominican-Style Braised Chicken Wings)

Makes 8 to 10 servings

These wings are inspired by pollo guisado, a dish that holds a special place in my heart, reminding me of the affordable, comforting meals I grew up with. Watching my mom cook pollo guisado alongside my grandma was pure joy—they'd be so happy, chatting and watching novelas while the dish simmered for hours, its soulful flavor slowly building. Those same tastes will be winners at your next game night, potluck, or Sunday table—perfect for feeding the whole squad.

- 3 pounds party-style chicken wings, skin-on
- 1½ cups Dominican-style sofrito (preferably Loisa brand), divided
- ¼ cup canola oil
- 2 small red onions, sliced
- ½ cup chopped garlic
- ¼ cup Maggi seasoning (or tamari)
- 3 tablespoons ground cumin
- 3 tablespoons lemon pepper seasoning
- 1 tablespoon smoked paprika
- 1 quart chicken stock, chicken broth, or vegetable stock
- ½ cup tomato paste
- Zest and juice of 2 oranges
- 7 Mezzetta Spanish Queen olives, pitted and chopped (or Castelvetrano olives)
- 1 stick (8 tablespoons) salted butter

Marinate the chicken wings in 1 cup of the sofrito in a sealed plastic bag for at least 3 hours or overnight. (Reserve the remaining ½ cup of sofrito for braising.)

Add the oil to a wide frying pan with a lid. Set over medium-high heat until it reaches 350°F on a thermometer. Working in batches, add the wings to the oil and fry for 2 to 3 minutes per side, until golden brown and crispy. The internal temperature of the wings should reach at least 165°F. Remove the wings from the pan and set aside on a paper towel–lined plate.

Reduce the heat to low, and add the onions and garlic to the same pan. Cook for 5 to 7 minutes, or until softened. Add the wings back to the pan, then add the Maggi seasoning, flipping the wings to coat them. Sprinkle in the cumin, lemon pepper, and smoked paprika.

Pour in the stock, bring to a simmer, then stir in the tomato paste, reserved ½ cup sofrito, orange zest and juice, and olives. Cover and braise over low heat for 30 minutes, until the meat is tender and easily pulls away from the bone. Transfer the wings to a serving platter. Stir the butter into the remaining sauce and cook until melted; then pour it over the wings. Serve immediately.

To store: If you plan to freeze the wings, stop before adding the sauce to them. Instead, store wings and sauce separately in airtight containers. Refrigerate for up to 4 days, or freeze for up to 3 months. Reheat together in a skillet over medium heat, adding a splash of stock or water to refresh the sauce if needed.

Special equipment

Oil thermometer

Pairing suggestion: La Loma (page 33) or To Die Dreaming (page 41)

Plátanos al Ron (Coconut Rum–Caramelized Sweet Plantains)

Makes 4 servings

In the Dominican Republic, as in much of the Caribbean and West Africa, ripe plantains are a staple—fried and served alongside savory dishes or transformed into dessert-like treats. This variation caramelizes sweet plantains in coconut rum, brown sugar, and cinnamon, intensifying their natural sugars while adding subtle tropical warmth. The result is a rich, silky snack or side that pairs beautifully with sweet and savory dishes. Whether served atop a scoop of coconut ice cream or alongside slow-cooked meats, these plantains are a celebration of the DR's love for bold tastes and indulgent textures.

- **2 to 3 tablespoons unsalted butter**
- **2 large ripe plantains (yellow with black spots), peeled and cut diagonally into ½-inch-thick slices**
- **¼ cup dark brown sugar**
- **½ teaspoon ground cinnamon**
- **½ teaspoon kosher salt**
- **2 tablespoons coconut rum (preferably RumHaven) or 2 tablespoons coconut water and ¼ teaspoon rum extract**
- **Lime zest, for garnish (optional)**

Melt 2 tablespoons of the butter in a large nonstick or cast-iron skillet over medium heat, 1 to 2 minutes, until fully melted and slightly foamy. Add the plantains in a single layer and cook for 2 to 3 minutes on one side, until the bottom turns deep golden brown with slightly crisped edges. The plantains should release easily from the pan when ready to flip. If they stick, let them cook another 30 seconds before trying again. Cook on the other side for 2 to 3 more minutes, adding the remaining 1 tablespoon butter as needed, until both sides are golden brown.

Sprinkle the brown sugar, cinnamon, and salt evenly over the plantains and let cook for about 1 minute, then gently flip to allow the other side to caramelize. Stir as needed to prevent burning—the sugar will melt and form a glossy coating.

Carefully pour in the coconut rum and let it bubble vigorously for about 1 minute, or until the liquid thickens slightly. Gently flip the plantains once or twice more, allowing the sauce to darken and fully caramelize, 1 to 2 more minutes. The plantains should be deep amber, glossy, and sticky.

Remove the plantains from the heat. Transfer to a serving dish, and pour any remaining sauce on top. Garnish with lime zest if desired, and serve hot.

Pairing suggestion: Candied Culture (page 35)

Yaniqueques

Makes 4 yaniqueques

Award-winning Afro-Dominican chef, author, and my friend Paola Velez generously shared her recipe for yaniqueques (photograph on page 37)—one of my favorite Dominican snacks sold at street corner stands in Washington Heights. Traditionally made from wheat flour, baking powder, and water, a yaniqueque is a type of fried bread often enjoyed plain, or with sweet or savory toppings. It is typically served as a snack with powdered sugar (sweet) or con ketchup (savory), or as an accompaniment to the classic Dominican dish *la Bandera* (rice, beans, and chicken).

- 1 cup all-purpose flour, plus more as needed
- ⅛ teaspoon baking soda
- ⅛ teaspoon baking powder
- ½ teaspoon kosher salt
- ¼ to ½ cup warm water, as needed
- Safflower oil, for frying
- Candied Yam Syrup (page 164) or Spiced Honey Syrup (page 162), for serving

Make the dough: In a medium bowl, combine the flour, baking soda, baking powder, and salt. Start by adding ¼ cup of warm water, mixing until the dough begins to come together. Add additional water, a tablespoon at a time, until a smooth dough forms. The dough should feel pliable but not sticky.

Transfer the dough to a clean, lightly floured work surface, and knead for about 5 minutes, or until it's smooth and elastic. Return it to the bowl, cover it with a kitchen towel and let rest at room temperature for 15 to 20 minutes.

Divide the rested dough into 4 equal portions. Transfer to a floured work surface, roll them into balls and then flatten into rounds, 5 to 6 inches in diameter.

Fry the yaniqueques: Add 1½ inches of safflower oil to a heavy pan set over high heat. Once the oil reaches 350°F on a thermometer, start adding the rounds in batches, ensuring they have enough space to cook evenly. Fry each round for about 1 minute per side, or until golden brown. Once fried, remove them from the oil and transfer to on a paper towel–lined plate. Serve the yaniqueques warm, topped with Candied Yam Syrup (page 164) or Spiced Honey Syrup (page 162).

Pairing suggestion: Santa Rosa (page 36)

Special equipment

Oil thermometer

FLORES, FRUTAS Y HIERBAS

FLORAL, FRUITY & HERBAL

COCKTAILS

63 **Navy & the Dock**
coconut gin, orgeat syrup, Green Chartreuse, lemon juice, black lemon bitters

64 **Zombie Reviver No. 2**
gin, banana rum, Cointreau, passion fruit liqueur, cream sherry

66 **Captain's Final Word**
spiced rum, Sorel Liqueur, Yellow Chartreuse, aromatic bitters, cinnamon, peppercorns, lime

67 **Coconut Daiquiri**
coconut rum, coconut liqueur, coconut syrup, lime

69 **Valdez Punch**
Cognac, blanco Tequila, IslandJon Apple Gwayav vodka, banana liqueur, ginger liqueur, Old Man Guavaberry Rum Liqueur, guava, banana syrup, ginger beer, lime

70 **Dulcito e Coco**
coconut vodka, elderflower liqueur, nigori sake, fresh lime juice, absinthe

72 **Bon Swa**
Haitian clairin, saffron-spiced liqueur, dry vermouth, mango nectar, white balsamic vinegar, Grains of Paradise

74 **Gracias Ancestros**
egg white, prickly pear & orange blossom gin, lime juice, Nixta Licor de Elote, corn coconut milk, corn husk honey water, pineapple tepache

BITES

76 **Homemade Plantain Chips with Culantro Garlic Salt**

77 **Herb-Infused Queso De Hoja with Honeyed Tropical Fruit**

79 **Dominican Chorizo "Kipe" Bites**

81 **Grilled Pineapple & Queso Blanco Skewers with Honey-Lime Glaze**

An Exploration of Flowers in Mixology

The term "botanicals" encompasses a wide range of plant parts used in cooking and mixology, including leaves, flowers, seeds (often in the form of spices), bark (such as cinnamon), fruit peels, roots, and even twigs. Whether cultivated or foraged, botanicals bring complex and nuanced flavors, aromas, and vibrant hues to cocktails, providing endless creative opportunities for mixologists.

Some botanicals are age-old, while other plants have only emerged recently in the world of cocktails, used for their flavors, fragrances, or natural colors. They can be enjoyed in cocktails as bitters, syrups, liqueurs, infusions, and even edible garnishes.

Floral infusions have timeless appeal, lending romance and delicacy to many cocktails, be it dandelion wine, honeysuckle vodka, or rose water (see Mayaimi Swizzle, page 145). These infusions—often made by steeping flowers in alcohol—are versatile additions, sometimes offering drinkers the sense of sipping a bouquet. When working with floral ingredients, I urge you to prioritize sustainably sourced and organic flowers—and try to ensure the same is true of any pre-made floral spirits you purchase.

Among the most striking of these floral ingredients is hibiscus, beloved for its tart, berry-like flavor profile and bright crimson hue. It is used around the globe—from the Caribbean to West Africa to Mexico to Polynesia—to infuse drinks with bold flavor. Its versatility shines in the Captain's Final Word (page 66), where Sorel Liqueur adds floral brightness to the deeper spiced notes.

Floral liqueurs, including elderflower, lavender, and hibiscus, are essential tools for mixologists. The delicately sweet St-Germain Elderflower Liqueur, made from fresh elderflowers (and used in Dulcito e Coco, page 70), is often credited with broadly reviving interest in the entire family of floral spirits.

Cocktails in this chapter embrace the broad spectrum of floral infusions and liqueurs, from saffron-spiced liqueur in Bon Swa (page 72) to the orange blossom–infused gin in Gracias Ancestros (page 74)—each one showcasing how floral ingredients enhance not only presentation but texture, flavor, and the drinking experience.

Herbs in Cocktails

Fresh herbs add aroma, complexity, brightness, and freshness to cocktails. The only stand-alone herb used in this chapter is mint, which shows up in Zombie Reviver No. 2 (page 64), Dulcito e Coco (page 70), and Cabana Rum Punch (page 87), where it helps lift the drink's tropical richness.

Other common cocktail herbs like cilantro and basil aren't major players in my recipes, but their bright, citrusy profiles often complement tropical fruits and spices behind the scenes. Falernum syrup and liqueur, infused with lime zest, clove, ginger, and almond, extend the reach of herbs and spices behind the bar. It appears in Rooted in Oakland (page 142), Mayaimi Swizzle (page 145), and the Over-the-Table Old Fashioned (page 146), adding warm, aromatic depth without pushing an overpowering freshness.

Herbaceous spirits, like Green Chartreuse—which is made with 130 botanicals—lay the groundwork for vivid, and intriguingly complex cocktails. Chartreuse is the star ingredient in the Last Conacado (page 101), where its bold profile goes head to head with Mezcal, chocolate, and citrus.

Many *amari* (plural of amaro) also derive their complexity from blends of herbs, roots, and flowers. They are highlighted in the chapter on bitters (see page 83), although their herbal foundations connect them to the broader tradition of plants as deliciously defining players in drinks.

The Fruity, Floral & Herbal Flavor Family

These are among the ingredients that bring fragrance, brightness, and freshness to the glass—petals, fruits, and tender herbs that lift, soften, or surprise, often in unexpected combinations. They're the gentle hand lending nuance to bold cocktails.

- anise
- apple mint, pineapple mint, peppermint
- berries
- citrus
- coconut
- elderberry
- hibiscus (sorrel, bissap, flor de jamaica)
- lavender
- manzanilla (chamomile)
- marjoram
- melon
- mint
- orange blossoms
- pineapple sage
- rose
- rosemary
- saffron
- thyme

Coconuts

Coconuts are a staple of Dominican and Caribbean culinary identity. The sweet, milky fruit (Yes, it's a fruit—not a nut!) is common in dishes from the region—so it might surprise you to learn that coconuts are not native to the Caribbean. It's believed they were brought to the region from West Africa by Spanish and Portuguese ships transporting enslaved people. Their electrolyte-rich water, nutrient density, and the plant's ability to thrive in sandy soil made coconuts invaluable to enslaved communities as well as plantation economies.

Today, coconuts are integral to dishes across the Caribbean—coconut water, oil, and milk remain prized for their versatility, appearing in savory stews and sweet treats alike. In Jamaica, coconut milk enriches rice and peas, curries, and soups; in Trinidad and Tobago, coconuts feature in *callaloo* (stew) and coconut bake (bread); in Barbados, they're used in desserts like sweet bread and coconut turnovers.

Navy & the Dock

Growing up in New York City, one of my favorite places to visit was Pier 86 on the Hudson River, home to the historic USS Intrepid. This cocktail draws on that memory—the Navy ship and the dock that anchored it—and from the broader legacy of port cities that shaped me: New York City, Douala in Cameroon, where my ancestors are from, and Santo Domingo in the Dominican Republic. These coastal hubs, each with its own rhythm, culture, and flavor, are the spirit behind this drink. It balances the creamy richness of coconut oil–washed gin with the herbal complexity of Green Chartreuse. Nutty orgeat syrup, bright lemon juice, and black lemon bitters add depth, while a subtle saline kiss evokes the sea.

If you can find Bimini Coconut Gin, I recommend grabbing a bottle. It is fat-washed with organic, Fair Trade Certified coconut oil, a process that infuses it with a natural coconut flavor. The distillers then chill the gin to remove the solidified oil, leaving behind a delicate coconut essence that perfectly complements its botanicals, including juniper, coriander, grapefruit peel, and chamomile. If Bimini Coconut Gin isn't available, the Chef's Note below offers an easy, homemade solution.

Chef's Note: To create coconut oil–washed gin, use the technique for Coconut Oil–Washed Scotch (see page 145), replacing the Scotch with London dry gin. To mimic the effect of black lemon bitters, lightly toast a lemon peel and shake it with the ingredients.

- **1½ ounces coconut oil–washed gin (such as Bimini, or see Chef's Note)**
- **½ ounce orgeat syrup**
- **½ ounce Green Chartreuse**
- **½ ounce fresh lemon juice**
- **3 dashes black lemon bitters (such as Scrappy's, or see Chef's Note)**
- **2 drops saline solution (page 20)**
- **Lightly toasted lemon peel, for garnish (see page 156)**

In a shaker, combine the gin, orgeat syrup, Green Chartreuse, lemon juice, bitters, and saline solution with cubed ice. Shake vigorously to chill. For a smooth texture, double strain into a chilled coupe. Garnish with a lemon twist, gently twisting the peel over the cocktail to release aromatic oils onto the surface of the drink. Place the expressed peel on the edge of the glass and serve immediately.

Special equipment

Fine-mesh cocktail strainer

Glassware

Chilled coupe

Ice

1 cup cubed (for shaking)

Zombie Reviver No. 2

This cocktail riffs on two legendary drinks—the tiki-style Zombie and gin-based Corpse Reviver No. 2, a classic "hair of the dog" cocktail popularized in Harry Craddock's *The Savoy Cocktail Book* published in 1930. The original "No. 2" is known for its crisp citrus and absinthe kick. Created at my Oakland bar, Sobre Mesa, this tropical take features Chinola liqueur for bright tang (*chinola* is the Dominican Spanish word for passion fruit), cream sherry for nutty depth, and Ron Colón Red Banana Oleo Rum for layered tropical richness. An absinthe spritz draws all the elements together for a crisp herbal finish.

1¼ ounces gin

1 ounce Ron Colón Salvadoreño Red Banana Oleo Rum

½ ounce Cointreau (or good-quality triple sec of your choice)

½ ounce Chinola Passion Fruit Liqueur

¾ ounce cream sherry (or Amontillado sherry)

½ ounce fresh lemon juice

½ ounce fresh lime juice

¼ ounce Demerara Syrup (page 165)

Absinthe spritz, for serving (see spirit spritz, page 22)

1 mint sprig, for garnish

1 dehydrated orange wheel (see page 155), for garnish

1 Amarena or brandied cherry, for garnish (optional)

In a shaker, combine the gin, rum, Cointreau, passion fruit liqueur, cream sherry, lemon juice, lime juice, and Demerara Syrup with cubed ice. Shake well and strain into a barrel mug. Top with crushed ice. Spritz absinthe over the drink, then garnish with a mint sprig, dehydrated orange wheel, and an Amarena or brandied cherry (if using).

Chef's Note: To substitute the Ron Colón Salvadoreño Red Banana Oleo Rum, use a lightly funky Jamaican rum plus ¼ ounce Combier Crème de Banane.

Special equipment	Glassware	Ice
Spray bottle or atomizer	Barrel mug	½ cup cubed (for shaking) plus ¾ to 1 cup crushed ice (for serving)

UNDERSTANDING SHERRY

Sherry is a fortified wine originally from Andalusia, Spain, made primarily from Palomino grapes and aged using the unique solera system. Styles range from bone-dry to richly sweet:

- **Amontillado:** starts dry, develops nutty richness with age
- **cream:** a sweetened blend, usually based on oloroso, with notes of dried fruit and toffee
- **fino and manzanilla:** crisp, dry, saline
- **oloroso:** rich, full-bodied, often oxidative and nutty

In cocktails like Zombie Reviver No. 2 (page 64) and Gingerbread Holiday Milk Punch (page 51), richer sherries such as oloroso and cream sherry balance spice, citrus, and spirits with a lush, velvety finish.

Captain's Final Word

Inspired by the classic Last Word cocktail, this Caribeño twist calls on spiced rum for warmth and depth. My first grab is Chairman's Reserve Spiced Original, artfully crafted in Saint Lucia with five-year and twelve-year rums spiced up with infusions of cinnamon, clove, nutmeg, allspice, citrus, and vanilla. Enriched by bois bandé, a bark native to Saint Lucia, it offers a deep earthiness that is ideal for sipping, cocktails, and even glazes and sauces. In the Captain's Final Word, the rum's aromatics perfectly complement the herbal Yellow Chartreuse, bright lime juice, and the subtle hint of cherry in the Sorel Liqueur. The bottom line is a bold tribute to the Last Word, infused with the spirit of the Caribbean.

1 teaspoon ground cinnamon

¼ teaspoon freshly ground black pepper

1 lime wedge

1 ounce Sorel Liqueur

1 ounce Yellow Chartreuse

1 ounce fresh lime juice

3 dashes Angostura bitters

2 drops saline solution (see page 20)

1 ounce spiced rum (preferably Chairman's Reserve, or homemade on page 158)

1 Amarena or brandied cherry (preferably Luxardo), for garnish (optional)

In a small bowl, combine the cinnamon and pepper. Pass the lime wedge all around the rim of the chilled coupe glass to wet it. Dip the rim into the spice blend.

In a shaker, combine the rum, Sorel Liqueur, Yellow Chartreuse, lime juice, bitters, and saline solution with the cubed ice. Shake vigorously, until the shaker is frosted on the outside and the drink is well chilled. Double strain the cocktail into the spice-rimmed coupe to achieve a smooth texture and clarity. If desired, garnish with an Amarena or brandied cherry on the edge of the glass or skewered inside. Serve immediately.

Chef's Note: This drink can be batched and refrigerated for up to 3 days. For best flavor, batch without the lime juice; then add lime juice just before serving to preserve brightness and prevent bitterness. Do not freeze.

Special equipment
Fine-mesh cocktail strainer

Glassware
Chilled coupe

Ice
1 cup cubed (for shaking)

Coconut Daiquirí

The Daiquiri, called a Rum Sour in its earliest days, is believed to have been invented in 1898 or thereabout. The story goes that Jennings Stockton Cox Jr., an American engineer working in Cuba at the time, was hosting guests near the port town of Daiquirí when his gin supply ran dry. He improvised with rum, lime juice, and sugar, and created an enduring classic in the process. This version pays due homage to the original, keeping its timeless structure intact and then adding a tropical twist. The cocktail features multiple layers of coconut flavor, thanks to RumHaven coconut rum, Kalani coconut liqueur, and coconut syrup to complement the lime's brightness.

- **1½ ounces RumHaven Coconut Rum**
- **½ ounce Kalani coconut liqueur, or other high-quality coconut liqueur (or more coconut syrup for a sweeter, richer version)**
- **½ ounce coconut syrup**
- **¾ ounce fresh lime juice**
- **2 drops saline solution (see page 20)**
- **1 lime wheel, for garnish**
- **Grated palm sugar, for garnish**

In a shaker, combine the rum, coconut liqueur, coconut syrup, lime juice, and saline solution with cubed ice. Shake vigorously for 20 to 30 seconds, until the shaker is frosted on the outside and the drink is well chilled. Use a fine-mesh cocktail strainer (in addition to the shaker's built-in strainer) to double strain the cocktail into a chilled glass. This ensures a smooth texture by removing ice shards and pulp.

To garnish, float a lime wheel on the surface and lightly sprinkle with grated palm sugar. Serve immediately.

Spirit-Free Coconut Daiquiri: Pre-chill the shaker and glassware to minimize dilution. Replace the coconut rum with 1½ ounces Abstinence Cape Spice and the coconut liqueur with ½ ounce sweetened coconut cream. Follow the rest of the recipe as written and serve immediately.

Chef's Note: This cocktail can be batched and refrigerated for up to 3 days. For best flavor, batch without the lime juice; then add fresh lime juice just before shaking and serving. Do not freeze.

Special equipment	Glassware	Ice
Fine-mesh cocktail strainer	Chilled coupe or Nick & Nora	1 cup cubed (for shaking)

GUAVABERRY LIQUEUR

This fruity liqueur holds a cherished place in Dominican culture and history. Made from the small, tart guavaberry fruit, which grows natively in the Caribbean, the liqueur is a vibrant symbol of tradition and community. Often enjoyed during Christmas and other festive occasions, its flavor is a tantalizing blend of sweet, tart, and spice.

The significance of guavaberry in the DR was immortalized by Juan Luis Guerra, the legendary Dominican musician and cultural icon, in his beloved song of the same name. In the Dominican Republic, guavaberry is not just a flavor—it's a connection to heritage, a taste of home, and a melody that carries the rhythm of the island's soul. Whether sipped neat (on its own), used in cocktails, or enjoyed in a dessert, guavaberry liqueur is a testament to the Caribbean's rich agricultural and cultural legacy.

Valdez Punch

Makes 15 (5-ounce) drinks

Valdez is the street in Oakland where AlaMar Dominican Kitchen—my first restaurant—was born. My dream came true there, and I named this punch after the street as a personal nod tribute to my journey. The drink is built around IslandJon, a Black-owned vodka brand that celebrates the apple guava, a fruit native to the Caribbean. Co-founder Levi John, who grew up in Trinidad and Tobago, found inspiration in his childhood memories of the floral aroma of guava trees. The banana component comes from Pairidaēza Crème de Banane, a liqueur made with ripe bananas and plantains for a sum total that's equal parts sweet and earthy.

- 750 mL Rémy Martin Cognac (or your favorite brand)
- 375 mL blanco Tequila
- 500 mL IslandJon Apple Gwayav vodka
- 450 mL Pairidaēza Crème de Banane liqueur
- 4 ounces The King's Ginger Liqueur
- 2 ounces Old Man Guavaberry Rum Liqueur
- 1 cup fresh lime juice, plus more to taste
- ½ cup guava nectar
- 2 ounces Spicy Guava Syrup (page 168)
- 2 ounces Banana Syrup (page 162)
- 2 (250 mL) bottles Fever Tree ginger beer, to top off
- 15 dehydrated lime wheels (see page 155), for garnish
- Dried hibiscus flowers, for garnish (optional)

In a large punch bowl or pitcher, combine the Cognac, Tequila, vodka, banana liqueur, ginger liqueur, guavaberry liqueur, lime juice, guava nectar, Spicy Guava Syrup, and Banana Syrup. Stir well until fully incorporated. Taste and adjust the lime juice for balance, adding more if needed to cut through the sweetness.

Just before serving, add the ice and gently pour in the ginger beer, stirring to combine. Ladle into punch glasses and garnish each serving with a lime wheel and a hibiscus flower.

Low-ABV Valdez Punch (one serving): Pre-chill the glass and ingredients. In a shaker, combine 2 ounces of Lustau Amontillado Sherry (18% ABV) or Carpano Bianco Vermouth (15% ABV) with ½ ounce of Lyre's White Cane Spirit (0% ABV) or Crodino (0% ABV), along with ½ ounce Banana Syrup (page 162), ½ ounce fresh lime juice, and ½ ounce guava nectar. Add 1 large ice cube and shake gently for 8 to 10 seconds, until the shaker is frosted on the outside and the drink is well chilled. Strain into a chilled Collins glass over fresh ice. Top with Fever Tree ginger beer, stir gently, and garnish with a lime wheel. Serve immediately.

Chef's Note: The base for both versions of this punch can be batched and refrigerated for up to 3 days. For best flavor, batch without the lime juice; then add it just before serving to preserve its brightness and prevent bitterness. Top with ginger beer at the time of serving. Do not freeze.

Pairing suggestion: Grilled Pineapple & Queso Blanco Skewers with Honey-Lime Glaze (page 81).

Special equipment	Glassware	Ice
Punch bowl or pitcher	Highball or punch glasses	4 to 6 cups cubed (for serving)

Dulcito e Coco FROM JULIAN ARREOLA

This cocktail is a testament to the artistry of guest bartender Julian Arreola, a Puerto Rican American raised in Chicago. With Dulcito e Coco, Julian reimagines the flavors of Puerto Rican coquito, a traditional holiday drink made with rum, coconut cream, and spices, offering a metropolitan twist that evokes the essence of urban tropics. In Julian's version, coconut-infused vodka, nigori sake, elderflower liqueur, and an absinthe rinse come together with fresh lime for a cocktail that is light, bright, and complex. Finished with a garnish of fresh mint and grated nutmeg, it's an ode to tropical flavors with a sophisticated edge, reflecting Julian's passion for honoring tradition while also innovating.

¾ ounce coconut-infused vodka (such as Cîroc Coconut or Absolut Coconut)

¾ ounce St-Germain Elderflower Liqueur

¾ ounce nigori sake (preferably Sho Chiku Bai)

½ ounce fresh lime juice

Absinthe, for rinsing (see page 22)

Mint sprig, for garnish

Freshly grated nutmeg, for garnish

In a shaker, combine the coconut vodka, elderflower liqueur, sake, lime juice, and cubed ice. Rinse the chilled glass by adding a small amount of absinthe, swirling to coat the interior, and discarding the excess. Shake vigorously for 20 to 30 seconds, until the shaker is frosted on the outside and the drink is well chilled, then double strain the cocktail into the glass. Garnish with a mint sprig and freshly grated nutmeg.

Low-ABV Dulcito e Coco: Pre-chill the shaker and glass to minimize dilution. Replace the coconut vodka with 1½ ounces Abstinence Cape Spice; omit the sake and absinthe rinse. Combine the Abstinence, elderflower liqueur (20% ABV), and lime juice in the shaker with ice. Shake gently for 8 to 10 seconds, until the shaker is frosted on the outside and the drink is well chilled. Strain into the chilled glass and serve immediately.

Pairing suggestion: Herb-Infused Queso de Hoja with Honeyed Tropical Fruits (page 77)

Special equipment
Fine-mesh cocktail strainer

Glassware
Chilled coupe or Nick & Nora

Ice
1 cup cubed (for shaking)

Herb-Infused Queso de Hoja
with Honeyed Tropical Fruit, page 77

Bon Swa

This cocktail takes its name from a word in Haitian Creole (Kreyòl Ayisyen, pronounced "kray-ol ah-yee-syen"). "Bon swa" is derived from the French phrase "bon soir," meaning "good evening." The name reflects a warm and casual greeting, in tune with the laid-back—yet still complex—nature of this cocktail. Haitian Creole, a rich blend of French, African, and other linguistic influences, embodies the essence of Haiti's Afro-Caribbean culture, and this drink honors that heritage with its lineup of ingredients. One standout is Grains of Paradise, a fragrant spice native to West Africa that resembles small peppercorns. Used here in tincture form, it offers a complex flavor profile with notes of cardamom, coriander, citrus, ginger, nutmeg, and juniper.

Chef's Note: Most commercial mango nectars contain added sugar, which balances tart ingredients in cocktails. If you're using an unsweetened version, you may want to adjust the amount of sweetener.

- **1¾ ounces Haitian clairin**
- **¼ ounce Apologue Saffron spiced liqueur**
- **½ ounce French-style dry vermouth (such as Noily Prat or Dolin Dry)**
- **½ ounce mango nectar (see Chef's Note)**
- **¼ teaspoon white balsamic vinegar**
- **Grains of Paradise tincture, for garnish (or freshly ground pink peppercorn)**

In a mixing glass, combine the clairin, saffron liqueur, vermouth, mango nectar, white balsamic, and the cubed ice. Stir for 30 seconds, until thoroughly chilled. Double strain the cocktail into the chilled glass. Garnish with two drops of Grains of Paradise tincture, or freshly ground pink peppercorn. Serve immediately.

Spirit-Free Bon Swa: Chill the mixing glass and serving glass in advance to minimize dilution. Replace the clairin with Abstinence Cape Floral, use a non-alcoholic dry vermouth, like Pentire Coastal Spritz or Ghia Apéritif. Replace the saffron liqueur with saffron syrup. Add to the mixing glass with mango nectar, white balsamic, and ¼ ounce Hibiscus Syrup (page 165). Fill with ice and stir gently for 8 to 10 seconds to combine. Give the mixture a second, brief stir just before pouring to ensure it is properly chilled. Double strain into the prepared glass. Garnish with freshly ground pink peppercorn.

Chef's Note: Both versions of this drink can be batched and refrigerated for up to 3 days. Do not freeze.

Special equipment
Fine-mesh cocktail strainer

Glassware
Chilled Nick & Nora

Ice
1 cup cubed (for stirring)

CLAIRIN

Clairin, or kleren, as it's known in Haitian Creole, has a deep, diasporic connection for Haitians and is almost always present at celebrations and ceremonies, such as Fèt Gede (Haiti's Day of the Dead, which takes place on November 1 and 2). During Fèt Gede, clairin is offered to both guests and the returning spirits of the dead.

Produced at hundreds of small distilleries across Haiti, clairin is a distilled alcoholic spirit made from sugarcane and processed similarly to rhum agricole and Brazil's cachaça. The pressed sugarcane juice is fermented using native yeast strains before being pot-still distilled, giving it a distinctive grassiness and raw, funky finish. Locally, clairin is often shipped in plastic jugs and sold in market stalls or by street merchants. Individual retailers add herbs or fruit to create unique flavor profiles.

A quick spotlight on just one of these merchants: In Port-au-Prince's underserved Cite Soleil neighborhood, sidewalk vendor Eddy Lecty and his father have been selling clairin for almost two decades in the same spot. Lecty spices his clairin with cloves, a twist that has gained a loyal following. Known as "The Citizens Club" by locals, Lecty's sidewalk stall has become a meeting place—even Haitian presidents have been known to visit.

Gracias Ancestros FROM ALEKA ROSS

Makes about 3½ to 4 cups, enough for 5 to 6 cocktails

Guest bartender Aleka Ross has spent over a decade educating, innovating, and storytelling. As an Indigenous Afro-Latina, Ross draws from her heritage to craft cocktails that honor tradition while embracing technique and innovation. In this cocktail, corn—a versatile staple crop across Africa, the Caribbean, and Latin America—takes center stage, showing up in Corn Coconut Milk, Nixta Licor de Elote, and Corn Husk Honey Water. All that corn is balanced out with Mexican Condesa gin and effervescent pineapple tepache.

> **Chef's Note:** Tepache is a traditional Mexican fermented drink made from pineapple peel and rind, piloncillo (Mexican unrefined cane sugar), and spices. It develops a bit of carbonation during the fermenting process. For store-bought tepache, look for a naturally carbonated brand, like De La Calle, typically available at specialty or Latin markets.

CORN HUSK HONEY WATER

- 4 to 5 corn husks (from organic corn)
- 4 cups water
- 1 ounce honey

- 1 egg white
- 2 ounces Condesa gin (preferably Prickly Pear and Orange Blossom, or another floral-style gin, such as Hendrick's or Bombay Sapphire East)
- 1 ounce fresh lime juice
- ¾ ounce Nixta Licor de Elote
- ¾ ounce Corn Coconut Milk (page 169)
- ¼ ounce Corn Husk Honey Water, plus more for garnish
- 2 ounces pineapple tepache, chilled

Make the corn husk honey water: Rinse the corn husks thoroughly. In a saucepot set over medium heat, combine the husks and water. Bring to a boil, then reduce the heat and simmer for 30 to 45 minutes. Remove and let cool completely. Strain and discard the husks; then stir the honey into the water until fully dissolved. Cool before using. Store in an airtight container in the refrigerator for up to 1 month.

Make the cocktail: In a shaker, combine the egg white, gin, lime juice, Nixta, Corn Coconut Milk, and Corn Husk Honey Water. Dry shake (without ice) vigorously for 20 to 30 seconds to build foam. Add the ice cubes and wet shake until the shaker is frosted on the outside and the drink is well chilled, about 30 seconds. Strain into a chilled highball glass, allowing space for the tepache. Let the cocktail rest for 30 to 45 seconds to allow the foam to settle. Slowly pour the pineapple tepache into the center of the foam to help it rise. Garnish with a drizzle of Corn Husk Honey Water.

Low-ABV Gracias Ancestros: Chill all ingredients and glassware in advance to minimize dilution. Replace the gin with Seedlip Garden 108, and omit the Nixta. Follow the method as written in the main recipe, beginning with the dry shake to build foam. Then add ice and wet shake only briefly—about 10 seconds—just until well chilled and lightly frothy. Follow the rest of the instructions to pour and garnish.

Glassware

Highball

Ice

4 cubes (for shaking)

Homemade Plantain Chips with Culantro Garlic Salt

Makes 6 to 8 servings

Golden, crisp, and herbaceous, these plantain chips are elevated by the bold, earthy flavor of culantro, a staple herb in many Dominican, Caribbean, and Latin American cuisines. Often confused with cilantro, culantro has a deeper, more robust aroma that shines in the garlic salt seasoning. These chips are perfect on their own or paired with dips, like my Caribbean–West African Red Bean Hummus (page 127).

Chef's Note: For the crispiest chips, slice the plantains as thinly and uniformly as possible. Select firm, green plantains for frying, as riper ones are too sweet and soft. Save any extra culantro garlic salt—it works wonderfully on roasted vegetables and grilled meats.

CULANTRO GARLIC SALT

¼ cup fresh culantro leaves, finely chopped

2 garlic cloves, minced

1 teaspoon kosher salt

PLANTAIN CHIPS

2 large green plantains, peeled and sliced into 1⁄16-inch rounds

Neutral oil for frying

Make the culantro garlic salt: In a small bowl, combine the culantro, garlic, and salt. Spread the mixture on a plate in a thin layer. Place the plate in a well-ventilated area and allow the salt mixture to air dry for 45 minutes to 1 hour, or until slightly dehydrated. Alternatively, dry the mixture in the oven on low heat (180 to 200°F) for about 10 minutes. Once dried, use a mortar and pestle or rolling pin to crush the mixture into a fine seasoning. Store in an airtight container at room temperature in a cool, dry place for up to 2 weeks.

Fry the plantain chips: Line a plate with paper towels. Heat 1 to 2 inches of neutral oil in a large, heavy skillet until it reaches 350°F. Working in small batches, fry the plantain slices in a single layer for 1 to 2 minutes per side, until golden and crispy. Use a slotted spoon to transfer the chips to the paper towel–lined plate to drain excess oil.

While the chips are still warm, sprinkle them with the culantro garlic salt and toss gently to coat. Serve immediately for the best texture and flavor.

Special equipment

Oil thermometer

Herb-Infused Queso de Hoja with Honeyed Tropical Fruit

Makes 6 servings

This vibrant family-style appetizer (photograph on page 71) features creamy queso de hoja, a traditional Dominican cow's milk cheese. The name *queso de hoja* translates to "leaf cheese," referring to its layered, stringy consistency that is similar to mozzarella. It is typically made by stretching and kneading curds into pliable layers, resulting in a cheese that is easily pulled apart. In this recipe, queso de hoja's mild, slightly salty taste and soft, elastic texture marry with the sweetness of tropical fruits and earthiness of fresh herbs.

Chef's Note: If queso de hoja is unavailable, queso blanco is an excellent substitute. Save any remaining herb-infused queso—it's delicious drizzled over salads and grilled vegetables.

HERB-INFUSED QUESO DE HOJA

- 1 pound queso de hoja
- 2 tablespoons olive oil
- 1 teaspoon fresh thyme leaves
- 1 teaspoon fresh oregano leaves
- ½ teaspoon cracked black pepper
- 1 garlic clove, thinly sliced

HONEYED TROPICAL FRUIT

- ½ cup fresh pineapple, diced
- ½ cup fresh mango, diced
- ¼ cup fresh papaya, diced
- ¼ cup passion fruit
- 2 tablespoons honey (preferably Caribbean or Nigerian wild-flower honey)
- 1 tablespoon fresh lime juice
- Pinch of kosher salt
- Fresh mint leaves, for garnish
- Toasted bread, crackers, or Homemade Plantain Chips (page 76), for serving

Make the herb-infused queso de hoja: Place the queso de hoja in a shallow casserole dish, ensuring it fits snugly with a little extra space around the edges. Set aside.

Special equipment

Oil thermometer

In a small saucepan, warm the olive oil over low heat, ensuring it does not exceed 200°F. Add the thyme, oregano, black pepper, and garlic, and cook until fragrant, stirring occasionally, about 2 minutes. Immediately pour the warm, infused oil over the cheese, ensuring all pieces are well coated. Cover the dish with a lid, plastic wrap, or cheesecloth, and refrigerate for at least 1 hour, or up to 24 hours, to allow the flavors to meld.

Make the honeyed tropical fruit: In a medium bowl, combine the pineapple, mango, papaya, and passion fruit. Drizzle with honey and lime juice, then add a pinch of salt. Gently toss to coat. Cover the bowl and refrigerate for at least 30 minutes.

Remove the cheese from the refrigerator 20 minutes before serving to bring it to room temperature. Arrange the cheese on a serving platter, spooning any remaining infused oil over the top. Surround it with the honeyed fruit and garnish with fresh mint leaves. Serve with toasted bread, crackers, or fried plantain chips.

Pairing suggestion: Dulcito e Coco (page 70)

Dominican Chorizo “Kipe” Bites

Makes 15 to 20 pieces

In the Washington Heights neighborhood of NYC where I grew up, instead of hot dog stands, we had stands that sold kipe and yaniqueques (see page 57). Kipe—pronounced *qui-peh*—is my mom’s favorite street food snack. It’s a Dominican adaptation of Middle Eastern kibbeh, brought to the island by Sephardic Jews in the nineteenth century. Over time, it has become a beloved part of Dominican *picadera* (appetizer) platters.

This version reimagines kipe with Afro-Caribbean chorizo and plantain masa, blending Dominican and West African flavors. While store-bought chorizo works, making your own isn’t too difficult, and adds depth of flavor well worth the extra step. This homemade chorizo stands apart from traditional versions, with a distinctive seasoning that includes Dominican oregano, culantro, and ají dulce.

Chef’s Note: Double the chorizo recipe and use the extra for breakfast sausage patties.

CILANTRO-LIME YOGURT

- 1 cup Greek yogurt
- ¼ cup chopped fresh cilantro
- 1 tablespoon wildflower honey (preferably Nigerian)
- Zest and juice of 1 lime
- 1 teaspoon kosher salt

AFRO-CARIBBEAN CHORIZO

- 2 ancho chiles, seeds and stems removed
- ¼ small yellow onion, minced
- 2 garlic cloves, minced
- 2 ají dulces (small, sweet peppers), finely chopped (see Chef’s Note, page 80)
- 1 teaspoon smoked paprika
- ½ teaspoon ground coriander
- ¼ teaspoon ground allspice
- 1 teaspoon ground cumin
- ½ teaspoon dried Dominican oregano (or regular oregano)
- 1 tablespoon kosher salt
- 1½ teaspoons distilled white vinegar
- 1 tablespoon finely chopped fresh culantro or cilantro
- ½ teaspoon dried thyme
- Pinch of freshly grated nutmeg (or ground nutmeg)
- 1 pound ground pork (75 to 80% lean)

KIPE BITES

- 1 batch Afro-Caribbean chorizo
- 1 tablespoon finely chopped fresh culantro or cilantro
- ¼ teaspoon freshly grated nutmeg (or ground nutmeg)
- ¼ teaspoon smoked paprika
- 1 recipe Plantain Masa Arepas dough (page 53), chilled for 30 minutes
- ½ cup fine cornmeal or breadcrumbs, for dredging (optional)
- Neutral oil, for frying
- Lime wedges, for serving

Make the cilantro-lime yogurt: In a small bowl, combine the yogurt, cilantro, honey, lime zest, lime juice, and salt. Stir the ingredients well until fully mixed. Cover the bowl and keep refrigerated until ready to serve.

CONTINUED

Special equipment

Oil thermometer, food processor

Make the ancho chile paste for the chorizo: Toast the ancho chiles in a dry skillet over medium heat until fragrant, 1 to 2 minutes per side. Transfer the toasted chiles to a bowl of warm water and allow them to soak for 15 minutes. Move them to the bowl of a food processor with 1 to 2 tablespoons of the soaking liquid and process to form a paste.

Make the chorizo: In a large bowl, combine the chile paste with the onion, garlic, ají dulces, paprika, coriander, allspice, cumin, oregano, salt, vinegar, culantro, thyme, and nutmeg. Stir to incorporate, then add in the ground pork and mix until fully blended. Refrigerate for at least 2 hours before cooking.

Set a large (10 to 12-inch) skillet over medium heat and add the chorizo. Cook, stirring occasionally, until browned and fully cooked through, 6 to 8 minutes.

Transfer the chorizo to a large bowl and add the culantro. Mix well and let cool to room temperature before continuing.

Make the kipe bites: Portion the chilled plantain masa arepas dough into balls about the size of a golf ball (roughly 2 inches wide). Using damp hands, flatten each ball into a ¼-inch-thick disc. Gently shape into small croquette-style bites—round or oblong, whichever you prefer. Place 1 teaspoon of the chorizo filling in the center of each disc. Carefully fold the masa around the filling, forming a mini-football shape and seal the edges completely. If desired, lightly roll each kipe bite in fine cornmeal or breadcrumbs before frying for extra crunch.

To pan-fry: Add ¼ inch of oil to a large skillet set over medium heat. Once the oil is shimmering, carefully add the kipe bites in batches, ensuring they are not overcrowded. Cook for 3 to 4 minutes on each side, or until golden brown and crisp. The edges should sizzle gently upon making contact with the oil—if they brown too quickly, reduce the heat slightly. Transfer to a paper towel–lined plate to drain excess oil.

To bake: Preheat the oven to 375°F. Brush each kipe bite lightly with oil, place on a sheet tray, and bake for 15 to 20 minutes, flipping halfway through, until the exterior is deeply golden and the center is firm when gently pressed with tongs.

Serve the kipe bites warm with cilantro-lime yogurt for dipping and lime wedges on the side.

Chef's Note: Ají dulce are small, sweet Caribbean peppers commonly used in Dominican and Puerto Rican cooking. Fresh (best when available), frozen, and dried ají dulce can be found at Latin or Caribbean markets and some farmers' markets. If using dried, rehydrate in hot water for 15 to 20 minutes, then remove the stems and seeds before chopping. Use about 1 tablespoon chopped rehydrated ají dulce in place of 2 fresh or frozen peppers, adjusting to taste. Jarred versions packed in vinegar are not recommended. For a shortcut, use fresh Mexican-style chorizo (raw, not cured). To capture the Afro-Caribbean flavors of this recipe, season it with a little allspice, coriander, smoked paprika, oregano, garlic, cilantro or culantro, and a pinch of nutmeg before cooking.

Pairing suggestion: Chan Chan (page 44)

Grilled Pineapple & Queso Blanco Skewers with Honey-Lime Glaze

Makes 6 to 8 skewers

Caribbean flavors thrive on contrast—sweet against savory, spice against citrus, heat against coolness. This dish brings it all together. The charred pineapple gets sweeter as it grills, its natural sugars caramelizing alongside the smoky edges of Dominican queso blanco, a mild, creamy cheese with a high melting point that allows it to hold its shape under heat. Honey-lime glaze ties everything together with brightness, warmth, and a touch of spice. In the Dominican Republic, grilled or roasted pineapple is often paired with cheese as a snack or dessert, making these skewers a perfect small bite to serve at a gathering.

Chef's Note: If using wooden skewers, be sure to soak them in water for at least ten minutes so they won't burn on the grill.

HONEY-LIME GLAZE

- 3 tablespoons honey
- 1 tablespoon fresh lime juice
- ½ teaspoon kosher salt
- ¼ teaspoon ground allspice

PINEAPPLE & QUESO BLANCO SKEWERS

- 2 cups fresh pineapple, cut into 1-inch cubes
- 8 ounces queso blanco, cut into 1-inch cubes
- 1 teaspoon neutral oil, for grill (optional)
- 2 tablespoons finely chopped fresh culantro or cilantro, for garnish

Preheat the grill to 450°F and lightly oil the grates to prevent sticking if needed. If using wooden skewers, soak them in water for 20 to 30 minutes.

Prepare the honey-lime glaze: In a small bowl, whisk together the honey, lime juice, salt, and allspice until smooth. Set aside.

Make the skewers: Thread the cubes of pineapple and queso blanco onto the skewers, alternating the pieces and making sure they're evenly spaced. Brush the skewers generously with the honey-lime glaze, reserving extra glaze for later.

Once the grill is hot, cook the skewers for 1½ to 2 minutes on each side, until the queso blanco develops light grill marks and the pineapple starts to caramelize and develop char marks. Brush the skewers with additional honey-lime glaze; then remove them from the grill.

To serve: Garnish the skewers with culantro or cilantro and serve immediately.

Pairing suggestion: Valdez Punch (page 69)

Special equipment

6 to 8 wooden (see Chef's Note) or metal skewers

AGRIA

SOUR & BITTER

COCKTAILS

87 **Cabana Rum Punch**
dark aged rum, sweet potato liqueur, ginger liqueur, allspice dram, almond extract, mango nectar, ginger juice, bitters, lemon/lime, mint

88 **The Latinidad Is Libre**
white rum, coconut water, lime juice, hibiscus syrup, mauby syrup, sour beer

91 **Tropical Noir**
rye whiskey, Orijin Bitters, plantain syrup, pineapple juice, Peychaud's bitters

93 **La Cultura Old Fashioned**
double barrel-aged rum, sweet potato liqueur, candied yam syrup, Angostura bitters

CHOCOLATE & COFFEE

95 **"Chocolate de Maní" Cocktail**
spiced rum, espresso, roasted peanut milk, vanilla, cinnamon

99 **Moka on the Table**
rye whiskey, coffee liqueur, plantain syrup, chocolate bitters, allspice bitters, espresso

101 **Last Conacado**
ancho chile-infused Mezcal, Green Chartreuse, crème de cacao, lime, grapefruit bitters

103 **Cafecito de la Mesa**
brandy, Amaro Montenegro, coconut cream, Demerara syrup, cinnamon, chicory pecan bitters, espresso

105 **Doña Rosa**
brandy, coffee liqueur, candied yam syrup, chicory pecan bitters, lemon juice, egg white

BITES

107 **Pickled Okra**

108 **Spicy Peruvian Ají Cashews**

109 **Green Mango & Cucumber Escabeche**

110 **Dominican Coffee Cake with Guavaberry Caramel Sauce**

Bitters: The Salt & Pepper of Cocktails

The word *cocktail* was first defined in print in 1806, tucked into a political newspaper item (the term appears in print as early as 1798, and mixed drinks and punches predate both)—and bitters were central from the start. They still are. Often called the bar's "salt and pepper," bitters enhance flavor, balance sweetness, and add complexity. These aromatic infusions—botanicals steeped in high-proof alcohol or glycerin—are used in small, potent amounts.

Despite the name, they don't necessarily make a drink bitter; they knit flavors together. Angostura tames Candied Yam Syrup in my La Cultura Old Fashioned (page 93); grapefruit bitters lift lime in the Last Conacado (page 101); and bitters deepen plantain syrup in Tropical Noir (page 91). Two icons—Angostura and Peychaud's—trace to the Caribbean and still shape cocktail culture.

Angostura Bitters

In 1824, Dr. Johann Gottlieb Benjamin Siegert developed the formula for Angostura bitters in Angostura, Venezuela (now called Ciudad Bolívar). While serving as Surgeon General under Simón Bolívar, Siegert perfected his "Amargo Aromatico" as a medicinal elixir for soldiers and sailors suffering from seasickness. By the 1850s, he began exporting to England, the Caribbean, and the United States, where his bitters gained popularity beyond the original medicinal use. In 1875, production was moved to Trinidad, where his sons launched the House of Angostura brand. Today, Angostura bitters continue to prove their worth; they are a key ingredient in my Cabana Rum Punch (page 87).

Peychaud's Bitters

Antoine Amédée Peychaud, a Creole apothecary born in Saint-Domingue (now Haiti), fled to New Orleans after the Haitian Revolution in 1791, between 1795 and 1796. In 1832, Peychaud opened a shop in the French Quarter and patented a signature blend of botanicals now known as Peychaud's bitters. His heady formulation of botanicals was key to the creation of the Sazerac, a cocktail that is still celebrated today. (For my take, see Tropical Noir, page 91.)

Bitter Spirits

Beyond aromatic bitters, bitter spirits such as Campari, Chartreuse, and various amari are essential for building modern cocktails that go deep and complex in the glass. Not at all shy, these spirits contribute herbal, citrus, and bittersweet undertones, balancing sweetness and acidity in drinks.

Amari are a large family of Italian herbal liqueurs made by infusing alcohol with herbs, spices, and citrus. Ranging from light to intensely bitter, they are sipped neat (straight pour, no ice), on the rocks, or in cocktails, like Last Conocado (page 101). Campari, a quintessential bitter liqueur, brings vibrant complexity to La Lucia (page 46), pairing its bold bitterness with hibiscus and tropical fruits. Producers like St. George Spirits and Amaro Angeleno incorporate ingredients like citrus, wildflowers, and herbs, creating versatile amari perfect for sipping or mixing into contemporary cocktails.

Aperitivo Cappelletti, key in the Dominican Date Sour (page 122), offers a softer bitterness with citrus-forward notes that perfectly complement the tamarind in the cocktail. In the Tropical Noir (page 91), Orijin bitters blaze a bold, herbaceous path, introducing earthy spice and citrus undertones that enhance rye whiskey's warmth.

Other notable bitter spirits include Cynar, an artichoke-based amaro with earthy, vegetal flavors, and Amaro Nonino, made distinct by nutty, herbal undertones offset by subtle sweetness. Fernet-Branca, known for its intense, medicinal bitterness, and Suze, a gentian-based aperitif with floral and earthy notes, are also solid choices for adding bold, bitter-forward intensity.

Sour Spirits, Infusions & Syrups

Sour flavors in cocktails typically originate from fresh citrus, but they can also come from sour spirits, infusions, and syrups. These elements introduce brightness and acidity, a refreshing contrast to sweet and bitter flavor structures.

Falernum syrup (featured in the Rooted in Oakland, page 142), with a blend of citrus and spice, exemplifies how effectively bitters and syrups can elevate cocktails. In Spice Me Down (page 117), soursop purée plays off of a splash of vinegar with spices for a uniquely complex cocktail.

Bitters remain indispensable, whether used sparingly or as a central component in a drink, transforming cocktails with subtle bitterness, depth, and layers of flavor.

The Sour & Bitter Flavor Family

The sour and bitter flavor family evokes sharpness and bite—whether from citrus, tamarind, or herbal bitters—delivering tension, freshness, and edge to a cocktail's structure.

- beer, sour beer
- bitters
- caramelized sugar
- citrus peel
- Dominican oregano, a.k.a. oregano de la isla
- grapefruit
- lemon, lime, and orange peel and zest
- pomegranate molasses
- slow-cooked alliums
- soursop
- tamarind
- tea
- walnuts
- yogurt
- vinegars

EQUIANO RUM

Born in 1745 into a prominent Igbo family in Nigeria, Olaudah Equiano was kidnapped as a child, sold into chattel slavery, and shipped to the Caribbean. Later transported to the UK, he gained freedom through determination and trading rum. Equiano wrote *The Interesting Narrative of the Life of Olaudah Equiano* (1789), becoming one of the first African authors published in the United Kingdom and the United States. His memoir detailed the horrors of the Transatlantic Slave Trade and became a cornerstone of the abolitionist movement.

Today, Equiano's legacy lives on through Equiano Rum, the world's first African-Caribbean blended rum. Founded in 2020 by Ian Burrell and Richard Seale, it combines rums from Gray's Distillery (Mauritius) and Foursquare Distillery (Barbados), mirroring Equiano's transatlantic trade route. Every element of Equiano Rum was designed with intention, resulting in a tightly woven concept that educates while paving the way for both progressive change and post-colonial rum production.

With no additives and a commitment to transparency, Equiano Rum honors its namesake's enduring impact while also promoting distillery justice and raising funds for Anti-Slavery International (ASI), the world's oldest organization dedicated to stopping human trafficking and fighting modern slavery.

Cabana Rum Punch

Makes 6 (4-ounce) servings

In my twenties, one of my favorite weekend party spots in New York City was the iconic Copacabana nightclub. It was there that I tasted the amaretto sour (my first actual cocktail after my usual rum and Coke), the drink that opened my eyes to a whole new world of flavors. "The Copa" was also the spot that inspired me, albeit years later, to get into the cocktail industry—I knew I wanted to create a space where people could come together, share great moments, and experience the same energy and excitement I felt every time I walked in. This Caribbean-inspired rum punch reimagines that first amaretto sour through a Caribbean lens, blending tropical flavors with the warmth of sweet potato (a staple of island cooking) and a subtle hint of almond.

Chef's Note: Most commercial mango nectars contain added sugar, which balances tart ingredients in cocktails. If you're using an unsweetened version, you may want to adjust the amount of sweetener.

- 6 ounces Equiano Rum (or your favorite aged dark rum)
- 3 ounces Corbin Cash Barrel Reserve Sweet Potato Liqueur
- 2 ounces The King's Ginger Liqueur
- 2 ounces St. Elizabeth Allspice Dram
- 2 drops almond extract
- 4 ounces mango nectar (see Chef's Note)
- 1 ounce ginger juice (such as The Ginger People brand)
- 8 dashes Angostura bitters
- 4 ounces fresh lemon or lime juice
- 12 mint sprigs, divided

In a non-reactive container, combine the rum, sweet potato liqueur, ginger liqueur, allspice dram, almond extract, mango nectar, ginger juice, bitters, and lemon juice. Bruise 4 mint sprigs (lightly press or slap them to release oils) and stir into the mixture. Cover and let the mixture infuse for at least 1 hour. Strain out and discard the bruised mint sprigs before proceeding.

Fill a large mixing glass with the cubed ice (if needed, work in two batches to avoid overfilling). Pour the punch mixture into the glass and stir for 20 to 30 seconds until well chilled and the outside of the glass is frosted. Strain into the rocks glasses over a large ice cube. Garnish each glass with a mint sprig. Serve immediately.

Chef's Note: This punch can be batched and refrigerated for up to 3 days. For best results, batch without citrus juice, adding it just before serving to preserve its brightness. Do not freeze.

Pairing suggestion: Green Mango & Cucumber Escabeche (page 109)

Special equipment

Muddler or long-handled spoon, fine mesh cocktail strainer

Glassware

Rocks

Ice

3 to 4 cups cubed (for stirring)
plus 1 large cube per glass (for serving)

The Latinidad Is Libre

I first tasted mauby soda while growing up in Washington Heights, where Dominican markets and restaurants kept it readily available. Mauby, a Caribbean drink made by boiling mauby tree bark with spices and sweeteners, is found in multiple forms: homemade, syrup, and bottled—still and carbonated. This cocktail is an ode to mauby, blending its deep, spiced complexity with coconut water and finishing with the crisp, refreshing lift of a sour beer float.

The origins of mauby trace back to the Indigenous Taíno people (who once inhabited Hispaniola), who brewed medicinal teas from local plants, including the bark that gives the drink its signature bittersweet flavor. Later, enslaved Africans in the Caribbean refined the preparation, incorporating fermentation techniques rooted in West African brewing traditions. These methods, originally used to create fermented grain- and fruit-based beverages, were adapted to local ingredients, resulting in an early version of mauby that was mildly alcoholic. Over time, the drink transitioned into the nonalcoholic spiced refreshment that's popular today, with notes of anise, cinnamon, and nutmeg that complement its distinct bitterness.

1½ ounces white rum

3 ounces coconut water

½ ounce fresh lime juice

½ ounce Hibiscus Syrup (page 165)

½ ounce mauby syrup (or use tamarind syrup plus 2 dashes of aromatic bitters such as Angostura or Peychaud's)

2 ounces sour beer, to float (see page 20)

Lime wheel, for garnish

Fill the glass with cubed ice. Pour in the rum, coconut water, lime juice, Hibiscus Syrup, and mauby syrup. Using a swizzle stick or barspoon, mix for about 7 seconds, until well incorporated. Float the sour beer over the top of the cocktail by slowly pouring it over the back of a spoon. Garnish with a lime wheel.

Chef's Note: This drink can be batched and refrigerated for up to 3 days in advance. For best flavor, batch without lime juice; then add lime juice just before serving to preserve brightness and prevent bitterness. Float sour beer on top just before serving. Do not freeze.

Glassware

Highball glass or barrel mug

Ice

1 cup cubed (for serving)

ORIJIN
BITTERS
SPIRIT DRINK

Tropical Noir

Tropical Noir is my Afro-Caribbean take on the Sazerac, a classic New Orleans cocktail made with rye whiskey or Cognac, Peychaud's bitters, and a sugar cube, served neat (on its own) in an absinthe-rinsed glass with a lemon peel garnish. I've blended the bold, spice-forward backbone of rye whiskey with Orijin Bitters for depth of flavor, along with unexpected richness from pineapple juice and plantain syrup. The traditional absinthe rinse adds layers of anise and herbal intrigue, while the bitters also nod to the classic version.

Chef's Note: Orijin Bitters is a Nigerian bitter liqueur made with traditional West African herbs and botanicals. It blends botanicals, roots, and fruits to create a bold, bittersweet profile with earthy, citrusy, and smoky back notes. Unlike typical cocktail bitters, which are used in small dashes, Orijin can be consumed as a standalone aperitif or incorporated into cocktails. If you can't find it, you can substitute ¼ teaspoon Angostura bitters plus ⅛ teaspoon St. Elizabeth Allspice Dram plus ⅛ teaspoon cinnamon syrup.

CINNAMON-CHARRED PINEAPPLE

1 fresh or canned pineapple ring

1 teaspoon brown sugar (optional)

½ teaspoon ground cinnamon

Absinthe, for rinsing (or use Pernod or Ricard)

2 ounces rye whiskey

½ teaspoon Orijin Bitters (see Chef's Note)

¼ ounce Plantain Syrup (page 166)

¼ ounce pineapple juice

2 dashes Peychaud's bitters

1 lemon twist (see page 156), for garnish

Make the cinnamon-charred pineapple: Drain the pineapple (if using canned) and pat as dry as possible with a paper towel. Dust the pineapple ring with brown sugar (if using) and ground cinnamon. Place under a broiler for 1 to 2 minutes per side, sear in a hot, dry skillet for 1 to 2 minutes per side or use a bartender's or chef's torch to char, until lightly caramelized. Cut a slit to use as a garnish and set aside.

Make the cocktail: Rinse the chilled rocks glass with absinthe and discard the excess. In a mixing glass, combine the rye whiskey, Orijin bitters, Plantain Syrup, pineapple juice, and Peychaud's bitters with 1 cup cubed ice. Stir until well chilled. Place a large ice cube in the prepared rocks glass. Double strain into the prepared glass. Garnish with a lemon twist and pineapple ring. Serve immediately.

CONTINUED

Special equipment	Glassware	Ice
Fine-mesh cocktail strainer	Rocks	1 cup cubed (for stirring) plus 1 large cube (for serving)

Tropical Noir, continued

Spirit-Free Tropical Noir: Pre-chill the mixing glass and rocks glass to minimize dilution. Replace the rye whiskey with 1½ ounces Abstinence Cape Spice and the Orijin bitters with ¼ ounce cinnamon syrup. Stir with ice until well chilled, then strain into the prepared glass. Express a lemon peel over the drink and discard before serving.

Chef's Note: While both the spirited and spirit-free versions can be batched, the absinthe rinse should be done directly in the glass when serving the boozy one. The bottle-batched spirit-free version can be refrigerated for up to 3 days. Add the lime juice just before serving to preserve brightness and prevent bitterness. Do not freeze.

Pairing suggestion: Green Mango & Cucumber Escabeche (page 109) or Dungeness Crab–Stuffed Piquillo Peppers (page 150)

La Cultura Old Fashioned

Corbin Cash Barrel Reserve Sweet Potato Liqueur is a one-of-a-kind creation. Corbin Cash distillery founder (and sweet potato farmer) David Souza found inspiration for the liqueur in his mother's recipe for sweet potato squares. Crafted from 100 percent estate-grown California sweet potatoes, the liqueur is distilled to a lower proof to preserve flavor and then aged in custom charred American white oak barrels for up to four years. All that plus a touch of brown sugar and some spices and extracts make it a rock-star start to this up-to-date old-fashioned cocktail.

1¼ ounces double barrel aged rum

¾ ounce Corbin Cash Barrel Reserve Sweet Potato Liqueur

½ ounce Candied Yam Syrup (page 164)

2 or 3 dashes Angostura bitters

1 marshmallow, candied yam slice (see page 155), or orange twist, for garnish (optional)

In a mixing glass, combine the rum, sweet potato liqueur, Candied Yam Syrup, and bitters with cubed ice. Stir for 20 to 30 seconds, until well chilled and the outside of the glass is frosted. Strain over a large ice cube in a rocks glass.

Skewer a marshmallow on a cocktail pick and toast it over a kitchen torch or gas stove flame until evenly browned. Garnish the drink by laying the toasted marshmallow skewer across the rim of the glass. Alternatively, garnish with a candied yam slice or an orange twist.

Glassware

Rocks

Ice

1 cup cubed (for stirring)
plus 1 large cube (for serving)

Chocolate & Coffee

From cacao to coffee, the Caribbean's two best-known bitter beans have shaped both resistance and ritual. Just as chocolate became a symbol of transformation, coffee has its own complex story of labor, legacy, and flavor.

Chocolate: A Bitter Past, a Bold Present

Cacao came to West Africa in the late 1800s by way of the Columbian Exchange, making it as Afro-Latino as any commodity. Although West Africa now produces up to 75 percent of the world's cacao, large quantities of cacao beans were grown in the Caribbean during the seventeenth and eighteenth centuries. Alongside sugar, cotton, and coffee, cacao formed the backbone of a plantation economy built by enslaved labor to enrich colonial powers like Britain, France, and Spain.

Cacao remains deeply embedded in Caribbean heritage, influencing traditional preparations and mixology. In cocktails like Last Conacado (page 101), the chocolate's richness and intensity are tempered with smoke or spice, evoking the complexity of Caribbean cacao traditions. From bitter roots in forced labor to its rebirth as a symbol of cultural identity, cacao tells a story of resilience and reinvention.

Coffee: From Revolution to Ritual

Coffee's origins trace back to Ethiopia, where popular lore tells of Kaldi, a herder whose goats danced after eating coffee berries. In 1720, French officer Gabriel de Clieu brought coffee to Martinique, and soon large plantations spread across the Caribbean. By 1788, Haiti supplied half of the world's coffee, fueling its economy (alongside sugar). Brutal conditions on these plantations were central to the Haitian Revolution in 1791.

To this day, Caribbean coffee remains an important crop. Jamaican Blue Mountain coffee, grown at elevations up to five thousand feet, is highly prized for its smooth, mild profile. To protect delicate seedlings from the sun, it is often cultivated alongside avocado and banana trees. Similarly, Dominican coffee is exclusively shade-grown, with guava and macadamia trees providing natural cover. Brands like Café Santo Domingo are known for their organic, hand-picked beans and sustainable farming practices.

In cocktails like Moka on the Table (page 99), Cafecito de la Mesa (page 103), and Doña Rosa (page 105), coffee's bold character is matched by spirits, liqueurs, and aromatic bitters in sync with its regional legacy. These drinks honor the bean's revolutionary roots in Caribbean ritual.

"Chocolate de Maní" Cocktail

Peanut milk lends this cocktail its creamy texture and nutty depth, paired with spiced rum and espresso for a rich, layered drink. Its name comes from the rhythmic street cry *"maní, maní"* still used by peanut vendors in the Dominican Republic, often with the *güira,* a traditional percussion instrument shown in the photo on page 97. In the Dominican Republic, "chocolate" often refers to hot milk-based drinks, not just cacao. While the classic version contains no chocolate, I've added just a hint in my Chocolate de Maní cocktail for balance and depth. Peanut milk itself has deep roots in West African cuisine, where peanuts are a staple, a tradition carried to the Caribbean through the Transatlantic Slave Trade and made integral to Afro-Caribbean foodways.

Chef's Note: Try adding a drop of toasted sesame oil to the cocktail shaker—it will amplify the nuttiness without overpowering the drink.

ROASTED PEANUT MILK

Makes about 2 cups

- ½ cup roasted unsalted peanuts
- 1½ cups warm water
- 1 teaspoon honey

- ½ ounce Spiced Honey Syrup (page 162), plus more for the glass
- 2 teaspoons crushed roasted peanuts, divided
- 1 ounce spiced rum (preferably Chairman's Reserve, or Clove-Infused Spiced Rum on page 158)
- ½ ounce crème de cacao
- 1 ounce freshly brewed espresso
- 1 ounce Roasted Peanut Milk
- ½ teaspoon vanilla bean paste (or seeds from half a vanilla bean)
- Pinch of cinnamon, plus more for dusting

Make the roasted peanut milk: In a blender, blitz the roasted peanuts, warm water, and honey for 1 to 2 minutes until smooth. Strain through a cheesecloth and store in the refrigerator in an airtight container for up to 5 days. Shake well before using, as natural separation may occur. (For a quick substitution if you're short on time, blend 2 tablespoons natural roasted peanut butter into ½ cup oat milk.)

Make the cocktail: Rim the glass with Spiced Honey Syrup, then dip it into half of the crushed roasted peanuts to coat. Set aside. In a shaker, combine the spiced rum, crème de cacao, espresso, peanut milk, Spiced Honey Syrup, vanilla, a pinch of cinnamon, and 1 cup cubed ice. Shake vigorously for 15 to 20 seconds, until the shaker is frosted on the outside and the drink is well chilled. Strain into the prepared glass filled with 1 cup fresh cubed ice. Sprinkle the remaining crushed peanuts evenly over the surface, and dust lightly with cinnamon. Serve immediately.

CONTINUED

Glassware	Ice
Highball	1 cup cubed (for shaking) plus 1 cup cubed (for serving)

"Chocolate de Maní" Cocktail, continued

Spirit-Free Chocolate de Maní: Pre-chill the shaker and glass to minimize dilution. Replace the spiced rum with Abstinence Cape Spice, the crème de cacao with ½ ounce of dark chocolate syrup such as Monin or Ghirardelli (or more to taste), and follow the main recipe as directed, but shake gently for only 8 to 10 seconds, until the shaker is frosted on the outside and the drink is well chilled. Serve immediately.

Frappé variation: In the carafe of a blender, combine all the cocktail ingredients (or the spirit-free ingredients) with 1½ cups of ice. Blend until the mixture is thick and creamy, with a texture similar to a coffeehouse-style frappé. Pour into a chilled glass, lightly dust the top with cinnamon, and serve immediately.

Pairing suggestion: Spicy Peruvian Ají Cashews (page 108)

PLANT-BASED MILKS & THE CARIBBEAN BAR

Dairy has never been the only path to creaminess. Across the Caribbean, bartenders and home cooks alike have long created "milks" from plants as essential building blocks of flavor and texture. These drinks carry quiet echoes of Africa, where nut, grain, and seed milks have nourished communities for centuries.

- **Macadamia Nut Milk:** Creamy, buttery, and lightly floral, macadamia milk brings unexpected elegance to cocktails. In La Loma (page 33), it gives body and roundness, much like groundnut milks in West Africa once did, though now reimagined with New World abundance.
- **Corn–Coconut Milk:** A fusion of two staples that traveled across oceans: maize, indigenous to the Americas, and coconut, carried by colonial trade routes, corn–coconut milk is both cozy and filled with sustenance. Together, they create a milk that appears in La Loma (page 33) and Gingerbread Holiday Milk Punch (page 51).
- **Roasted Peanut Milk:** Deeply Afro-diasporic at heart, roasted peanut milk is made from groundnuts (also known as peanuts), which were introduced to the Caribbean from Africa. It has since became a foundation for countless dishes and drinks, including the Chocolate de Maní (page 95).

And beyond . . . Coconut, almond, and cashew milks remain iconic across the region, appearing in punches and holiday drinks from Jamaica to Puerto Rico. Their presence recalls African practices of coaxing creaminess from plants, a wisdom that crossed the Middle Passage and thrived in new lands. Each plant milk stirred into a glass tells a story—of Africa, of the Caribbean, and of the diasporic creativity that binds them together.

Moka on the Table

Inspired by the coffee made in my mom's old-school Moka pot, this is not your favorite barista's mocha cappuccino! In many coffee-producing countries—and the Dominican Republic is no exception—it is normal to give children what I'd call a warm coffee-flavored milk. Coffee's natural bitterness is disguised with generous portions of milk and sugar (or condensed milk), making it a delicious sweet treat—the best part of my childhood breakfasts. The smell of coffee brewing still takes me back there. This is my grown-up take on that memory—bracing, bittersweet, and steeped through with flavors that call forth the warmth and the ritual of those early mornings.

Chef's Note: To bring a touch of floral brightness and extra depth to the drink, add a dash of Peychaud's bitters just before serving.

- **1½ ounces rye whiskey**
- **½ ounce coffee or espresso liqueur**
- **¼ ounce Plantain Syrup (page 166)**
- **2 dashes chocolate bitters**
- **1 dash allspice bitters (such as Dale DeGroff's Pimento Aromatic Bitters)**
- **1 shot (1½ ounces) freshly brewed espresso (preferably from a Moka pot)**
- **Chocolate shavings, for garnish (preferably Dandelion Zorzal Comunitario)**

In a cocktail shaker, combine the rye whiskey, coffee liqueur, Plantain Syrup, chocolate bitters, allspice bitters, espresso, and cubed ice. Shake vigorously for 20 seconds to create optimal foam. Double strain into the chilled coupe. Garnish with chocolate shavings—I recommend using a zester to grate fresh chocolate over the top.

Spirit-Free Moka on the Table: Pre-chill a shaker and glassware to minimize dilution. Replace the rye whiskey with 1½ ounces Abstinence Cape Malt, the coffee liqueur with ½ ounce more of the espresso, and the chocolate bitters with ½ ounce of dark chocolate syrup such as Monin or Ghirardelli (or more to taste). Shake gently for 15 seconds, and follow the rest of the instructions as written.

Pairing suggestion: Dominican Coffee Cake with Guavaberry Caramel Sauce (page 110)

Special equipment	Glassware	Ice
Fine-mesh cocktail strainer	Chilled coupe	1 cup cubed (for shaking)

Last Conacado

This cocktail is a liquid salute to CONACADO, a pioneering Dominican cacao cooperative that, starting in the 1980s, helped establish the country as a global leader in high-quality, fair-trade cacao and continues to provide support to small farmers. While many farmers have since transitioned to new export partnerships, the name acknowledges their foundational role in the Dominican cacao story. This recipe is a nod to that story, with a garnish of shaved Dominican chocolate that uplifts the smoky Ancho Chile–Infused Mezcal, herbal Chartreuse, vibrant lime, and crème de cacao for a rich yet still bright celebration of flavor.

While any high-quality Dominican chocolate works, I'm partial to Dandelion Chocolate's Zorzal Comunitario, which is made from cacao sourced from Reserva Zorzal, a farm and sanctuary in the Dominican Republic that dedicates 70 percent of its land to a bird sanctuary, supporting the country's commitment to sustainability.

1½ ounces Ancho Chile–Infused Mezcal (page 157)

½ ounce Green Chartreuse

½ ounce crème de cacao

½ ounce fresh lime juice

2 dashes grapefruit bitters

Shaved Dominican chocolate, for garnish (preferably Dandelion Zorzal Comunitario)

In a shaker, combine the Ancho Chile–Infused Mezcal, Chartreuse, crème de cacao, lime juice, and grapefruit bitters with cubed ice. Shake vigorously for 10 to 15 seconds, until the shaker is frosted on the outside and the drink is well chilled. Strain into the chilled coupe. Garnish with shaved Dominican chocolate and serve immediately.

Spirit-Free Last Conacado: Pre-chill the shaker and coupe to minimize dilution. In a shaker, combine 1 ounce Ritual Zero Proof Tequila Alternative, ½ ounce green tea syrup, ½ ounce chocolate syrup (like Monin or Ghirardelli), ½ ounce fresh lime juice, ¼ ounce Guajillo Chile Agave Syrup (page 167), and 1 teaspoon grapefruit juice. Add ice and shake gently for 8 to 10 seconds, until well chilled. Strain into the chilled coupe, express a grapefruit peel over the drink, and discard the peel. Garnish with shaved Dominican chocolate (as in the original version) and serve immediately.

Chef's Note: Both versions of this drink include citrus juices, but they can still be batched and refrigerated for up to 3 days. For best results, add the citrus juices just before serving to preserve its brightness. Do not freeze.

Glassware

Chilled coupe

Ice

1 cup cubed (for shaking)

CHARTREUSE

The origins of Chartreuse trace back to a 1605 manuscript gifted to the Carthusian monks by François Annibal d'Estrées, containing a detailed, complicated recipe for an "Elixir of Long Life." After over a century of refining the formula, the monks began producing the liqueur in 1737 at the Grande Chartreuse monastery in the French Alps. With 130 botanicals, the recipe remains a closely guarded secret, known only to two or three monks at a time.

Green Chartreuse: With 55% ABV, it offers an intense herbal and spicy profile with hints of mint, pine, and anise.

Yellow Chartreuse: Milder at 40% ABV, it has a sweet, soft profile with honeyed, floral, and saffron notes.

Both versions are naturally colored by the ingredients themselves, with no artificial additives.

Fun fact: The color "chartreuse" is named after the liqueur, not the other way around! The bright yellow-green hue of Green Chartreuse inspired the naming of the color in the late nineteenth century.

Cafecito de la Mesa

Sitting with my mom after family dinners, sipping rich, comforting Café Bustelo and talking about school and life are my fondest memories from growing up. These days, I love drinking coffee from Mr. Espresso, a roaster here in Oakland—especially the custom blend it created for Sobre Mesa. This cocktail, like my coffee rituals, is a reflection of both tradition and evolution. Cafecito de la Mesa blends the warmth of brandy, the nuttiness of coconut, and the spice of cinnamon with the punchy strength of espresso to create a drink that's as comforting as it is complex. A splash of Amaro Montenegro offers hints of orange blossom and warm spice, echoing the Dominican love of bold coffee flavors.

- **1½ ounces brandy**
- **½ ounce Amaro Montenegro**
- **½ ounce coconut cream**
- **½ ounce Demerara Syrup (page 165)**
- **¼ teaspoon ground cinnamon**
- **2 dashes chicory pecan bitters**
- **1 ounce freshly brewed espresso**
- **Burnt orange peel, for garnish**

In a mixing glass, combine the brandy, Amaro Montenegro, coconut cream, Demerara Syrup, cinnamon, chicory pecan bitters, and espresso. Stir to combine, then pour over a large ice cube in a rocks glass.

Make the burnt orange peel garnish: Cut a wide strip of orange peel, avoiding the pith. Briefly pass the peel over an open flame until lightly charred and aromatic.

Hold the citrus peel over the drink and quickly twist it to release the aromatic oils onto the surface of the cocktail. Run the peel around the rim of the glass before placing it in the drink. Serve immediately.

Spirit-Free Cafecito de la Mesa: Pre-chill the mixing glass and glassware to minimize dilution. Replace the brandy with 1½ ounces Abstinence Cape Spice; omit the Amaro Montenegro. For a spirit-free substitute for the chicory pecan bitters, use 1 tablespoon strong brewed chicory coffee (such as Café du Monde) mixed with 1 to 2 drops pecan extract or maple syrup. Combine the ingredients, including the espresso, as directed in the main recipe and stir gently for 10 to 30 seconds to combine. Refrigerate for at least 2 hours and up to 3 days. For best results, stir with ice just before serving to ensure proper dilution and texture.

Glassware

Rocks

Ice

1 large cube (for serving)

Doña Rosa

Growing up in Washington Heights, with a mom who worked two jobs, I spent a lot of time with the *tías*—the aunties—who kept an eye on me when my mother was out. Aunties were aunties, whether blood-related or not. Doña Rosa was one of them. Her tiny apartment always smelled like roasted coffee, caramelized plantains, and candied yams, and stepping inside felt like a warm embrace. Doña Rosa had a way of mixing sweetness with discipline. If you were good, you got a guava-stuffed marshmallow from the tin she kept by the window—soft, sticky, and melt-in-your-mouth.

This cocktail is a tribute to Doña Rosa, and to all the tías who raised us. Brandy provides a rich, steady foundation, while coffee liqueur echoes Doña Rosa's ever-present café. A final nod to the treats she gave us, a guava-dipped marshmallow sits on top, because every hard lesson learned deserves a sweet reward!

Chef's Note: For a touch of floral brightness and extra depth, add a dash of Peychaud's bitters alongside the chicory pecan bitters.

- 1½ ounces brandy
- ½ ounce coffee liqueur (preferably St. George NOLA Coffee Liqueur)
- ½ ounce Candied Yam Syrup (page 164)
- 3 dashes chicory pecan bitters
- ½ ounce fresh lemon juice
- 1 egg white or 2 drops cocktail foamer (see page 20)
- 1 guava-dipped marshmallow per glass, for garnish (optional, see page 156)

If using egg white: In a cocktail shaker, combine the brandy, coffee liqueur, Candied Yam Syrup, chicory pecan bitters, lemon juice, and egg white—don't add the ice yet. Dry shake vigorously for about 15 seconds to emulsify. Then add 4 ice cubes and wet shake for 10 to 15 seconds, until well chilled and frothy.

If using cocktail foamer: In a shaker, combine the brandy, coffee liqueur, Candied Yam Syrup, chicory pecan bitters, lemon juice, and cocktail foamer with 4 ice cubes. Wet shake vigorously for 15 to 20 seconds, until well chilled and frothy.

Strain into the chilled coupe, and garnish with a skewered guava-dipped marshmallow balanced on the edge of the glass if you'd like.

Low-ABV Doña Rosa: Pre-chill the glass and shaker to avoid dilution. Replace the brandy with 1½ ounces of Sorel Liqueur (15% ABV) and replace the coffee liqueur with 1 ounce of strong brewed espresso or cold brew concentrate, sweetened to taste. Follow the rest of the instructions as written. Shake gently for only 8 to 10 seconds, until the shaker is frosted on the outside and the drink is well chilled.

Chef's Note: Both the regular and low-ABV version of this drink can be batched and refrigerated for up to 3 days. For best results, add the lemon juice and egg white just before serving to preserve freshness.

Glassware

Chilled coupe

Ice

4 cubes (for shaking)

Pickled Okra

Makes about 1 quart

Pickled okra is part of a culinary lineage that connects Africa, the Caribbean, and the Americas. Native to West Africa, okra was carried to the Caribbean and the Americas through the Transatlantic Slave Trade, where it became an essential ingredient in Afro-Caribbean and Southern cooking. Its versatility and resilience made it a staple in stews, soups, and pickles. The technique of pickling—preserving foods in vinegar or brine—also has African roots, a practical (and flavorful) way to extend the life of fresh produce.

Throughout the Caribbean, pickled vegetables are common accompaniments to rich and spicy dishes, their acidic tang cutting through richer flavors with a clean, tangy profile. In this recipe, okra pods are infused with a vibrant blend of Caribbean-inspired spices that pays homage to their journey and enduring legacy.

Chef's Note: Instead of okra, try using 1 pound of yuca, peeled and cut into batons or coins. First, boil the yuca in salted water until fork-tender (10 to 15 minutes), drain, and cool. Proceed with the recipe as written.

- 1 orange, thinly sliced
- 4 sprigs fresh oregano
- 1 pound fresh okra, washed and patted dry
- 2 teaspoons mustard seeds
- 1 teaspoon whole black peppercorns
- 2 teaspoons whole cumin seeds
- 1 tablespoon whole allspice berries
- 2½ cups apple cider vinegar
- ¼ cup honey

Divide the orange slices and oregano among the jars. Use a paring knife to make ½-inch incisions on each okra pod, taking care to leave them whole. Pack the okra snugly into the jars over the orange slices and oregano.

In a small pot over medium-low heat, toast the mustard seeds, black peppercorns, cumin seeds, and allspice, stirring constantly, until fragrant, 2 to 3 minutes. Add the vinegar and honey, stir to incorporate, and continue cooking until the mixture is bubbling. Reduce the heat to low and simmer for 5 minutes. Look for wisps of steam and small bubbles forming around the edges of the pot. The spices should release a warm, toasty aroma, and you should see a glossy surface with a few slow-rising bubbles—this means the liquid is ready.

Pour the hot pickling liquid into the jars, ensuring the okra is fully submerged. Let cool to room temperature, then seal the jars. Refrigerate for at least 2 days before serving. The pickles will keep in the refrigerator for up to 2 weeks.

Pairing suggestion: Last Conacado (page 101)

Special equipment

Sanitized Mason jars (1 quart, 2 pints, or 4 half-pints)

Spicy Peruvian Ají Cashews

Makes 2 cups

These snackable, frankly addictive cashews bridge the flavors of Latin America and the Caribbean. The earthy heat of ají amarillo powder, balanced with smoky paprika, cumin, and a hint of garlic, transforms plain cashews into a bold, citrusy treat. A squeeze of fresh lime at the end brightens the spices, giving them a tangy kick—perfect with a cocktail or as a pre-dinner bite. These are the kind of bar snacks that disappear before the second round.

- 1 teaspoon ají amarillo powder
- 1 teaspoon smoked paprika
- ½ teaspoon ground cumin
- ½ teaspoon garlic powder
- ½ teaspoon kosher salt
- ⅛ teaspoon cayenne pepper (or more to taste)
- 2 cups raw cashews (or a mix of cashews and peanuts)
- 1 tablespoon neutral oil
- Juice of 1 to 2 limes (preferably limón criollo)

Make the ají seasoning: In a small bowl, combine the ají amarillo powder, smoked paprika, cumin, garlic powder, kosher salt, and cayenne pepper. Mix thoroughly and set aside.

Preheat the oven to 350°F. Line a baking sheet with parchment paper or a silicone mat. In a medium bowl, toss the cashews with neutral oil until evenly coated. Add in the ají amarillo seasoning and toss to distribute.

Spread the seasoned nuts in a single layer on the prepared baking sheet. Roast for 10 to 12 minutes, stirring halfway through. Watch carefully toward the end to avoid burning.

Remove the cashews from the oven and drizzle with fresh lime juice to taste while still warm. Once the nuts are cool enough to handle, serve them fresh. Store leftovers in an airtight container at room temperature for up to 2 weeks.

Pairing suggestion: "Chocolate de Maní" Cocktail (page 95) or Bidi Bidi Bom Bom (page 121)

Green Mango & Cucumber Escabeche

Makes about 3 cups

Pickling—a technique deeply rooted in West African culinary tradition—traveled by way of enslaved Africans, eventually influencing Caribbean and Latin American cuisine. Mangoes—though not indigenous to the Dominican Republic—have become a staple of the island's food culture, thriving in its tropical climate. Here, unripe mangoes, paired with cucumbers, lend a tart, crisp bite to Afro-Caribbean escabeche. An infusion of hot Scotch bonnet pepper, citrus, vinegar, and warm spices ensures that it's anything but shy in flavor.

- 1 large unripe green mango (10 to 12 ounces), peeled and julienned
- 2 Persian cucumbers, thinly sliced (or ½ English cucumber, seeded and sliced)
- 1 teaspoon kosher salt
- ½ cup apple cider vinegar
- ¼ cup sour orange juice (or 2 tablespoons fresh lime juice plus 2 tablespoons fresh orange juice)
- 2 garlic cloves, smashed
- 1 small Scotch bonnet pepper, halved (see Chef's Note)
- ½ teaspoon ground cumin
- ½ teaspoon ground coriander
- 3 whole allspice berries
- 1 bay leaf

In a large bowl, toss the green mango and cucumber with the salt. Let them sit for 15 minutes to draw out excess moisture and slightly soften. Drain off the released liquid and pat the mango and cucumber dry with paper towels. Set aside.

Next, make the brine. In a small saucepan over medium heat, combine the apple cider vinegar, sour orange juice, garlic, Scotch bonnet pepper, cumin, coriander, allspice, and bay leaf. Bring the mixture to a gentle simmer (do not allow it to boil), then turn off the heat and let it steep for 5 minutes. At this point, if you'd like less heat, discard the Scotch bonnet.

While the brine is still warm, pour it over the mango and cucumber mixture and toss to coat everything evenly. Let the mixture sit at room temperature until cool. Once cooled, transfer to an airtight container and refrigerate for at least 2 hours for the best flavor, but ideally 2 days.

Enjoy the escabeche chilled or at room temperature. Store in the refrigerator for up to 2 weeks, making sure the mixture remains fully submerged in the brine.

Chef's Note: Always wear gloves when handling Scotch bonnet peppers.

Pairing suggestion: Cabana Rum Punch (page 87) or Tropical Noir (page 91)

Dominican Coffee Cake with Guavaberry Caramel Sauce

Makes one 9-inch cake or 12 to 14 cupcakes

This tender, richly flavored cake (photograph on page 105) is inspired by my family's tradition of enjoying coffee cake in the morning before we go to visit my aunt and uncle in New Jersey. Its aromatic layers combine the bold intensity of coffee with a crunchy, buttery macadamia nut topping. Drizzled with guavaberry caramel sauce, it's a decadent, flavor-packed showstopper. Whether served as a full cake or individual cupcakes, this versatile treat is perfect for entertaining or indulging in a special moment.

TOPPING

- **½ cup all-purpose flour**
- **4 tablespoons (½ stick) unsalted butter, cold and cubed**
- **⅓ cup packed brown sugar**
- **1 to 1½ teaspoons espresso powder**
- **¼ cup macadamia nuts, chopped**

CAKE

- **1½ cups all-purpose flour**
- **1½ teaspoons baking powder**
- **3 eggs, whites and yolks separated**
- **½ cup powdered sugar**
- **1⅔ cups granulated sugar**
- **½ cup (1 stick) unsalted butter, softened, plus more for greasing**
- **¼ teaspoon fine sea salt**
- **1 teaspoon vanilla bean paste**
- **¼ teaspoon ground allspice**
- **½ teaspoon coffee extract**
- **½ cup whole milk**

GUAVABERRY CARAMEL SAUCE

Makes about 1½ cups

- **1 cup granulated sugar**
- **¼ cup water**
- **½ cup heavy cream**
- **2 tablespoons Old Man Guavaberry Rum Liqueur**
- **3 tablespoons unsalted butter**
- **Pinch of fine sea salt (optional)**

Preheat the oven to 350°F and position a rack on the center shelf. For a cake, grease a 9-inch round baking pan and line the bottom with parchment paper. For cupcakes, line a cupcake pan with cupcake liners.

Make the topping: In the bowl of a food processor, combine the flour, butter, brown sugar, and espresso powder. Process for 20 to 30 seconds, until the mixture resembles coarse crumbs and begins to clump together. Add the macadamia nuts, then pulse for 10 to 20 seconds, until a slightly sticky, coarse mixture forms. Refrigerate the crumble topping while you prepare the cake batter.

Make the cake: In a medium bowl, sift together the flour and baking powder and set aside. In the bowl of a stand mixer fitted with the whisk attachment, combine the egg whites and powdered sugar and whisk on high speed until stiff peaks form, 3 to 5 minutes. Transfer to a separate bowl and set aside.

Special equipment

Food processor, 9-inch cake pan or standard cupcake pan, stand mixer

Switch to the paddle attachment (no need to clean the bowl) and add the egg yolks, granulated sugar, butter, salt, vanilla paste, allspice, and coffee extract. Cream the mixture on medium speed until light and fluffy, 3 to 5 minutes. Reduce the speed to low, then add half of the flour mixture and half of the milk and mix lightly, just to combine. Use a rubber spatula to scrape down the sides of the bowl and repeat with the remaining flour mixture and milk, mixing just until combined. The batter should look smooth and evenly mixed, but still light and slightly fluffy. Avoid overmixing, which can make the cake dense. Gently fold in the whipped egg whites in two additions. Take care not to overmix, which will cause the batter to deflate.

To make a cake: Pour the batter into the prepared baking pan and spread the chilled topping evenly over the surface. Bake for 40 to 45 minutes or until a toothpick inserted in the center comes out clean. Transfer the pan to a wire rack to cool for 15 minutes then unmold. Remove from the pan and cool completely.

To make cupcakes: Divide the batter evenly among the cupcake liners, filling each about two-thirds full. Sprinkle the chilled topping evenly over each portion of batter. Bake for 18 to 22 minutes, or until a toothpick inserted in the center comes out clean. Transfer the pan to a wire rack and cool for 10 minutes. Carefully remove the cupcakes from the pan to the rack and cool completely.

Make the guavaberry caramel sauce: In a medium, heavy saucepan, combine the sugar and water. Set over medium heat, stirring gently but often until the sugar dissolves completely, 2 to 3 minutes. Let the mixture come to a boil and then boil undisturbed for 8 to 10 minutes—it will turn a deep amber color. Watch closely to prevent scorching, and if needed, gently swirl the pan to ensure even caramelization, but avoid stirring constantly—this may cause the sugar to crystallize.

Once the mixture is deep amber in color, reduce the heat to low. Slowly pour in the heavy cream, stirring continuously. The mixture will steam and bubble vigorously. Once the bubbling subsides, stir in the guavaberry liqueur, mixing thoroughly; then add the butter, stirring until melted and fully incorporated, 1 to 2 minutes. Carefully taste the caramel, and if desired, add a pinch of salt to balance the sweetness. Let the caramel sauce cool slightly before serving or transferring to a jar or container. Store in the refrigerator for up to 2 weeks. Rewarm the sauce before serving.

Once the cake or cupcakes are cool, drizzle with the guavaberry caramel sauce and serve.

Pairing suggestion: Santa Rosa (page 36) or Moka on the Table (page 99)

PICOSO

SPICY

COCKTAILS

117 **Spice Me Down**
coconut rum, blended aged rum, pear nectar, lime, soursop purée, Alma Tepec Chile Pasilla Liqueur, guajillo chile agave syrup, cinnamon, nutmeg

118 **My Familiar**
Tequila, ancho chile-infused Mezcal, dry orange curaçao, mango nectar, orange shombo shrub, limón criollo juice, guajillo chile agave syrup, lime, jerk pepper bitters

121 **Bidi Bidi Bom Bom**
Mezcal, Alma Tepec Chile Pasilla Liqueur, yuzu sake, pineapple juice, lime, watermelon shrub, Demerara syrup

122 **Dominican Date Sour**
whiskey, tamarind, bitter aperitivo liqueur, Amaro Montenegro, orange suya-spiced agave, lime

125 **Fair & Hotter**
rhum agricole, sweet vermouth, Cointreau, habanero bitters, orange suya-spiced agave, yerba maté spiced honey, lime

126 **República 75**
vodka, tamarind, lemon, cayenne, guava cider

BITES

127 **Caribbean-West African Red Bean Hummus with Tostones**

130 **Afro-Cuban Mojo Olives with Peanuts**

131 **Dominican Ahi Tiradito**

132 **Spicy (Picoso) Ají Amarillo Shrimp & Yuca Skewers**

Bring on the Heat: Using Chiles in Cocktails

Chiles have long been celebrated for their versatility—and their ability to radically transform culinary experiences. Bold heat and surprisingly complex flavor profiles make them an exciting addition to cocktails. Once primarily associated with savory dishes, chiles now also take center stage in syrups, shrubs, liqueurs, and infused spirits.

Infusions with Impact

Spicy infusions are easy to make at home and endlessly customizable, allowing for experimentation with different peppers and chiles, infusion times, and flavor combinations. This book features a few, like Spicy Guava Syrup (page 168) and Guajillo Chile Agave Syrup (page 167), which both lend depth and heat to cocktails without overwhelming the palate. These infusions achieve a careful balance of sweet, smoky, and spicy, exemplified in drinks like Spice Me Down (page 117) and My Familiar (page 118). The latter also includes Orange Shombo Shrub, an infusion made with the smoky, moderately spicy West African shombo chile.

Bottled Heat: Spirits & Liqueurs

The use of chile-infused spirits is on the rise, from artisanal producers to home bartenders. Mezcal brands like Del Maguey Vida, or homemade infusions like Ancho Chile–Infused Mezcal (page 157), featured in My Familiar (page 118), offer smoky depth with a sweet, mellow spice. Habanero-infused Tequilas and vodkas bring fire to spicy margaritas and Bloody Marys, while Alma Tepec Pasilla Chile Liqueur, featured in Bidi Bidi Bom Bom (page 121), showcases the smoky essence of pasilla peppers—perfect for citrus-forward or herbal cocktails.

Balancing the Burn

Adding chiles to cocktails draws out multidimensional flavor that enhances but doesn't overpower. For example, Fair & Hotter (page 125) showcases the earthy complexity of rhum agricole, brightened with citrus and given a fiery edge with habanero bitters.

Balance is paramount when crafting chile-infused drinks. Too much heat can overwhelm the palate, but just enough allows other flavors to shine.

Chiles pair especially well with sweet or acidic elements—like the pear nectar and soursop purée in Spice Me Down (page 117)—creating harmony between heat and flavor. From the gentle heat of Yerba Maté Spiced Honey (page 160) to the smoky depth of a pasilla liqueur, chiles remain one of the most versatile and exciting ingredients in modern cocktail making.

The Spicy Flavor Family

Heat in cocktails isn't just about fire—it's about flavor. From chile tinctures to spiced syrups, the picoso (spicy) flavor family plays with balance, using spice to amplify depth, sweetness, and complexity.

- chiles (fresh, dried, and pastes, including habanero, serrano, ancho, Scotch bonnet, ají dulce, ají amarillo)
- garlic
- ginger
- hot paprika
- mustard seeds or mustard powder
- peppercorns (black, white, pink, Sichuan, Grains of Paradise)
- spicy bitters (including habanero bitters, Jamaican jerk bitters)
- suya spice blend (also called yaji)
- Tajín seasoning

Spice Me Down

The name comes straight from the playful Caribbean expression "spice me down," which is often used to describe being deliciously overwhelmed by bold flavor, warmth, or even attraction—just like this cocktail. It leans into lush Caribbean flavors with a mix of coconut rum, aged rum, and tropical fruit. Soursop purée and pear nectar give it a creamy-tart mouthfeel, with lime juice keeping it bright. Garnished with pineapple fronds and a brandied or Amarena cherry, it's playful, aromatic, and unmistakably tropical.

Chef's Note: If fresh soursop isn't available, look for frozen soursop pulp in Latin American, Caribbean, or Asian grocery stores—it's often labeled *guanábana*. Choose unsweetened pulp when possible. To make the purée, thaw the pulp and blend until smooth, aiming for a thick, pourable consistency similar to mango nectar. Add a small splash of water or coconut water only if needed to loosen the texture. Strain for a finer result, if desired. Avoid pre-sweetened versions, which may affect the drink's balance. Store any extra purée in the refrigerator for up to 3 days or freeze in portions.

1 ounce RumHaven coconut rum

1 ounce blended aged rum (such as Planteray Barbados 5 Year or Diplomático Mantuano)

1 ounce pear nectar

¾ ounce fresh lime juice

½ ounce soursop purée plus ¼ ounce water, mixed well (see Chef's Note)

½ ounce Alma Tepec Chile Pasilla Liqueur

⅛ ounce Guajillo Chile Agave Syrup (page 167)

Pinch of ground cinnamon

Pinch of ground nutmeg

2 pineapple fronds, for garnish

1 Amarena or brandied cherry, for garnish

1 orchid flower, for garnish (optional)

In a cocktail shaker, combine both rums, the pear nectar, lime juice, prepared soursop purée, Alma Tepec liqueur, Guajillo Chile Agave Syrup, cinnamon, and nutmeg with cubed ice. Shake vigorously for 10 to 15 seconds, until the shaker is frosted on the outside and the drink is well chilled.

Strain into a Collins glass filled with fresh cubed ice. Garnish with pineapple fronds, an Amarena or brandied cherry speared on a bamboo pick, and an orchid flower if desired. Serve immediately.

Spirit-Free Spice Me Down: Pre-chill the shaker and glass to minimize dilution. Replace the coconut rum with ½ ounce sweetened coconut cream; replace the blended aged rum with 1½ ounces Abstinence Cape Spice. Replace the Alma Tepec with ¼ ounce additional Guajillo Chile Agave Syrup. Combine with all other ingredients as directed in the main recipe. Shake gently for 8 to 10 seconds to combine, then strain into the chilled glass filled with fresh ice. Garnish as above and serve immediately.

Pairing suggestion: Caribbean–West African Red Bean Hummus with Tostones (page 127)

Glassware	Ice
Collins	1 cup cubed (for shaking) plus 1 cup cubed (for serving)

My Familiar

In many spiritual traditions, especially African, Caribbean, and Latin American, a "familiar" (pronounced fah-mee-LEE-ahr) refers to a spiritual companion or guide—mystical, powerful, and grounding. The name My Familiar nods to that idea. With a beguiling mix of citrus, sweetness, and smoke, it captures something bold, unforgettable, even a little bit magical. This recipe combines bright Tequila with smoky Ancho Chile–Infused Mezcal—both of them complemented by tropical mango nectar and a complex Orange Shombo Shrub. Dry orange curaçao ties the flavors together with its zesty, bittersweet character and crisp, dry finish.

Chef's Note: For a bolder spice profile, add ½ teaspoon ground Grains of Paradise along with the shombo in the shrub.

ORANGE SHOMBO SHRUB
Makes about 2 cups

- 1 cup fresh orange juice (from 3 to 4 oranges)
- 1 tablespoon grated orange zest
- ½ cup apple cider vinegar
- ½ cup Demerara sugar
- 1 teaspoon ground shombo (or dried cayenne pepper or African bird's eye chile)
- 1-inch piece fresh ginger, thinly sliced

- Creole seasoning, for half-rim
- 1 ounce reposado Tequila
- 1 ounce Ancho Chile–Infused Mezcal, homemade (page 157) or store-bought
- ½ ounce dry orange curaçao
- ½ ounce Orange Shombo Shrub, or ½ ounce fresh lemon juice mixed with a few drops of hot sauce and a tiny pinch of ground ginger)
- ¾ ounce limón criollo juice (or fresh Key lime juice)
- ½ ounce Guajillo Chile Agave Syrup (page 167)
- 8 to 10 drops jerk bitters (see Chef's Note)
- Chile-infused dehydrated blood orange wheel (see page 155), for garnish

Make the orange shombo shrub: In a small saucepan over medium-low heat, combine the orange juice, orange zest, vinegar, sugar, shombo, and ginger. Stir until the sugar fully dissolves, then bring to a gentle simmer. Cook for 5 more minutes, stirring occasionally, until the mixture is aromatic and gently bubbling around the edges. Remove from heat and let cool to room temperature.

Transfer the shrub to a clean glass jar. Seal tightly and refrigerate for at least 24 hours to allow the flavors to develop. After 24 hours, strain the shrub through a fine-mesh sieve or cheesecloth into a clean bottle, discarding the solids. Store in the refrigerator for up to 2 weeks.

Special equipment

Large fine-mesh strainer or cheesecloth

Glassware

Double rocks

Ice

1 cup cubed (for shaking) plus 1 cup cubed (for serving)

Make the cocktail: Rim half of a double rocks glass with Creole seasoning. In a shaker, combine the Tequila, Mezcal, curaçao, Orange Shombo Shrub, limón criollo juice, Guajillo Chile Agave Syrup, and jerk bitters with cubed ice. Shake vigorously for 10 seconds, until the shaker is frosted on the outside and the drink is well chilled Strain into the glass over fresh cubed ice. Garnish with a dehydrated blood orange wheel.

Chef's Note: If jerk bitters are unavailable, substitute 2 dashes Angostura bitters and 1 or 2 dashes of mild hot sauce (such as Crystal or Cholula).

CURAÇAO

Curaçao, along with its neighbor Aruba, was settled around AD 1000 by the Caquetío, an Arawak people who migrated from Venezuela. The Spanish colonized Curaçao in 1499, and in 1515, enslaved the entire Indigenous population and sent them to Hispaniola (the island that includes Haiti and the Dominican Republic). Today, Aruba, Bonaire, and Curaçao form the "ABC islands," all autonomous countries within the Kingdom of the Netherlands.

Unsurprisingly, the island is home to the eponymous liqueur. Curaçao the *liqueur* is made by macerating the dried peels of the laraha—an intensely sour citrus fruit with orange notes native to Curaçao—in a neutral spirit or brandy base, often aged with spices to lend subtle warmth and depth of flavor. While the blue curaçao variety is sweeter (and artificially colored), dry orange curaçao offers a more refined, nuanced, not-too-sweet profile and a distinct orange hue.

Popular curaçao brands such as Pierre Ferrand Dry Curaçao highlight a refined, slightly brandy-like character, which makes it a useful ingredient in classic cocktails like the Mai Tai and El Presidente. For substitutions, Cointreau or Grand Marnier can provide a similar citrus brightness, though with varying levels of sweetness.

Bidi Bidi Bom Bom FROM ALEJANDRO ARRIAGA

Named in tribute to Selena—the iconic Mexican-American singer whose hit song "Bidi Bidi Bom Bom" still resonates across generations—this cocktail is both playful and deeply personal for guest bartender Alejandro Arriaga, whose passion, resilience, and commitment to creating a sense of belonging shine through in every pour. Born into a Mexican immigrant family, Alejandro had to navigate the challenges associated with growing up undocumented, eventually finding confidence through boxing and a creative outlet in the restaurant industry. His refreshing, summery cocktail uses watermelon shrub, balanced out by crisp citrus and tangy tamarindo chamoy.

Chef's Note: If you can't find yuzu sake, substitute nigori sake plus a splash of fresh yuzu or lemon juice.

WATERMELON SHRUB

Makes 1 to 1¼ cups

2 cups diced watermelon

½ cup sugar

½ cup apple cider vinegar

Tamarindo chamoy, for rimming the glass

2 ounces Mezcal

1 ounce Alma Tepec Chile Pasilla Liqueur

1 ounce yuzu sake (preferably Hojun, or see Chef's Note)

1 ounce fresh pineapple juice

¾ ounce fresh lime juice

½ ounce Watermelon Shrub

¼ ounce Demerara Syrup (page 165)

Classic Mexican watermelon candy, such as Vero Sandía or Pulparindo Sandía, for garnish

Pineapple fronds, for garnish

Make the watermelon shrub: In a medium bowl, combine the watermelon and sugar. Let macerate at room temperature for 1 to 2 hours, until the sugar dissolves and the watermelon releases its juice. Strain through a fine-mesh strainer into a second clean bowl, pressing lightly to extract as much liquid as possible without pushing pulp through the strainer. Stir in the apple cider vinegar. Transfer the mixture to a sterilized jar and refrigerate for up to 2 weeks.

Make the cocktail: Rim the Collins glass with tamarindo chamoy. In a shaker, combine the Mezcal, Alma Tepec, yuzu sake, pineapple juice, lime juice, watermelon shrub, and Demerara Syrup with crushed ice. Shake vigorously for 15 seconds, until the shaker is frosted on the outside and the drink is well chilled. Strain into the prepared glass over crushed ice. Skewer the Mexican watermelon candy or place it directly on the rim. Add a pineapple frond for a tropical touch. Serve immediately.

Pairing suggestion: Spicy Peruvian Ají Cashews (page 108)

Special equipment	Glassware	Ice
Large fine-mesh strainer	Collins	1½ cups crushed (for shaking) plus 1½ cups crushed (for serving)

Dominican Date Sour

Tamarind is sometimes called the "Dominican date"—and in fact, the word *tamarind* likely derives from the Arabic word *Tamar-u'l-Hind* (date of India). It's true that tamarind pulp and dried dates share a similar texture, although unlike the candy-sweet date, tamarind has more of a sour-sweet flavor that makes it great for cocktails. This cocktail puts tamarind at center stage, balancing it with warm whiskey and complex, herbal amaro. The combination of tamarind, whiskey, Aperitivo Cappelletti, and lime creates a layered, citrus-forward profile.

2 ounces whiskey (such as bourbon or rye)

½ ounce tamarind paste purée

1 ounce Aperitivo Cappelletti

½ ounce fresh lime juice

½ ounce simple syrup (see page 20)

½ ounce Amaro Montenegro

¼ ounce Orange Suya–Spiced Agave (page 161)

Guava slice, for garnish

In a shaker, combine the whiskey, tamarind paste purée, Aperitivo Cappelletti, lime juice, simple syrup, Amaro Montenegro, and Orange Suya–Spiced Agave with cubed ice. Shake vigorously for 10 to 15 seconds, until the shaker is frosted on the outside and the drink is well chilled. Strain (or for a smoother texture use a fine-mesh strainer to double strain) into the chilled coupe. Garnish with the guava slice. Serve immediately.

Chef's Note: This drink can be batched and refrigerated for up to 3 days. For the best flavor, batch without lime juice; then add lime juice just before serving to preserve brightness and prevent bitterness. Do not freeze.

Pairing suggestion: Ají Amarillo Shrimp & Yuca Skewers (page 132)

Special equipment

Fine-mesh cocktail strainer (optional)

Glassware

Chilled coupe

Ice

1 cup cubed (for shaking)

Afro-Cuban Mojo Olives with Peanuts, page 130

Fair & Hotter

This cocktail is a hot, spicy take on the classic Fair & Warmer, which is itself a rum-based riff on a Manhattan. It combines a bold and complex fusion of flavors, with grassy, herbaceous rhum agricole balanced by sweet Cointreau, rich vermouth, and fiery habanero bitters. Orange Suya–Spiced Agave introduces a West African influence, adding smoky, nutty warmth that deepens the interplay of heat and citrus. This subtle but high-impact twist makes for a nuanced drink that celebrates shared culinary traditions between Africa and the Caribbean.

1½ ounces rhum agricole

¾ ounce sweet vermouth (preferably Dolin Vermouth Rouge)

½ ounce fresh lime juice

¼ ounce Cointreau (or good-quality triple sec of your choice)

¼ ounce Orange Suya–Spiced Agave (page 161)

¼ ounce Yerba Maté Spiced Honey (page 160)

3 dashes habanero bitters

Dehydrated lime wheel (see page 155), for garnish

In a shaker, combine the rhum agricole, vermouth, lime juice, Cointreau, Orange Suya–Spiced Agave, Yerba Maté Spiced Honey, and habanero bitters with cubed ice. Shake vigorously for 10 to 15 seconds, until the shaker is frosted on the outside and the drink is well chilled. Strain into the chilled coupe. Garnish with a dehydrated lime wheel and serve immediately.

Low-ABV Fair & Hotter: Replace the rhum agricole with 1 ounce Lustau Amontillado sherry and ½ ounce Ritual Zero Proof Tequila Alternative. Swap the Cointreau for ¼ ounce nonalcoholic orange aperitif, such as Lyre's Orange Sec. Shake gently for 8 to 10 seconds, until the shaker is frosted on the outside and the drink is well chilled. Follow the rest of the recipe as written.

Chef's Note: The low-ABV version can be batched and refrigerated for up to 3 days in advance. For best flavor, batch without lime juice; then add lime juice just before serving to preserve brightness and prevent bitterness. Do not freeze.

Pairing suggestion: Afro-Cuban Mojo Olives with Peanuts (page 130)

Glassware

Chilled coupe

Ice

1 cup cubed (for shaking)

República 75

This cocktail is a vibrant, Dominican-inspired take on the French 75, a classic concoction made with gin, Champagne, lemon juice, and sugar and that, by some accounts, dates back to World War I. For the República 75, I use vodka as a base, and add sweet-tart tamarind, lemon, a pinch of cayenne, and top it off with the effervescent snap of guava cider. Finished with a Tajín-dusted lemon wheel, this refreshing, citrusy sparkler brings together sweetness, spice, and acidity. It's a celebration of flavors that come from all over the world yet remain deeply Caribbean.

1½ ounces vodka (preferably Tito's)

1 ounce tamarind paste purée

1 ounce fresh lemon juice

Pinch of cayenne (optional)

Guava cider such as Shacksbury Guava or Ace Guava Cider, to top off (2 to 3 ounces)

1 (⅛-inch) lemon wheel, for garnish

Tajín seasoning, for garnish

In a shaker, combine the vodka, tamarind paste purée, lemon juice, and cayenne (if using) with cubed ice. Shake vigorously for 10 to 15 seconds, until the shaker is frosted and the drink is well chilled. Strain into the chilled flute. Slowly and gently float the guava cider into the glass over the back of a spoon to top off the cocktail, being careful to prevent overflow or loss of carbonation.

To make the garnish: Dab the lemon wheel with a paper towel to remove moisture, then sprinkle one side with Tajín or dip just the edge, for a subtler effect. Use immediately, or let dry slightly on a parchment-lined tray.

Garnish the cocktail with the Tajín-dusted lemon wheel. Serve immediately.

Spirit-Free República 75: Pre-chill the shaker and flute to minimize dilution. Replace the vodka with Optimist Bright Zero Proof Vodka and the guava cider with a nonalcoholic sparkling guava drink of your choice. Follow the main recipe to combine the ingredients, then shake gently with ice for 8 to 10 seconds. Follow the rest of the instructions as described above.

Chef's Note: The base for both versions of this drink can be batched and refrigerated for up to 3 days in advance. Batch without the lemon juice and sparkling guava cider (or soda); then add them just before serving to preserve its carbonation. Do not freeze.

Glassware

Chilled flute

Ice

1 cup cubed (for shaking)

Caribbean–West African Red Bean Hummus with Tostones

Makes 4 to 6 servings

Beans are a staple in West African and Caribbean cuisines, with legumes like black-eyed peas, cowpeas, and kidney beans central to many traditional dishes. They're versatile, affordable, and nutritious, providing essential protein, fiber, and vitamins. This party-ready recipe combines earthy West African–style red beans with Dominican sazón, toasted sesame seeds, bright Meyer lemon, and a touch of cayenne heat. The final dish is puréed into a hummus-style dip and served with classic Dominican *tostones* (fried, flattened green plantains).

Chef's Note: For best flavor and texture, I recommend using high-quality dried beans. Sort through to remove any grit or debris, then rinse well before cooking—no soaking needed. If you prefer to soak your beans, 8 hours or overnight will do the trick.

If you don't own a plantain smasher, place the fried plantain slices between wax or parchment paper and flatten them using a heavy-bottomed glass or a can from your pantry.

- ½ cup dry, small, red beans or kidney beans (see Chef's Note)
- 2 cups vegetable stock, plus more as needed to cover the beans
- 2 tablespoons tomato paste
- ½ cup toasted sesame seeds
- ½ cup finely chopped red onion
- ¼ cup chopped cilantro
- 5 garlic cloves, minced
- 1 tablespoon Old Bay seasoning
- 1 teaspoon ground cumin
- 2 teaspoons Dominican sazón (preferably Loisa brand)
- ¼ teaspoon ground cayenne pepper
- Zest and juice of 2 Meyer lemons
- Kosher salt

TOSTONES

- 1 teaspoon kosher salt
- 4 cups water
- 2 green plantains, peeled and cut into 1½-inch discs
- Canola oil, for frying (2 to 3 inches in a frying pan)

Cook the beans: In a large pot, combine the beans, vegetable stock, and tomato paste, stirring to dissolve the tomato paste. Bring to a boil over medium heat, then reduce to a simmer. Leave the pot uncovered, and cook until the beans are very soft. Timing will vary depending on the type and size of bean. Start testing small red beans at about 45 minutes and larger ones at 1 hour. Add warm water or additional stock as needed to keep the beans fully submerged during cooking. About half the liquid should remain at the end, slightly thickened from the starches released during simmering.

Stir in the sesame seeds, red onion, cilantro, garlic, Old Bay, cumin, sazón, and cayenne. Simmer over medium-low heat for 10 minutes, stirring occasionally until the onions soften. Remove from the heat and let cool for 10 to 15 minutes before blending.

CONTINUED

Special equipment

Blender or food processor, oil thermometer, plantain smasher (see Chef's Note)

Make the hummus: Using a slotted spoon, transfer the beans to a blender or food processor. Reserve the cooking liquid. Add the lemon zest and juice. Blend, gradually adding the cooking liquid 1 tablespoon at a time, until smooth and creamy. You'll need ½ to ¾ cup of cooking liquid total, depending on your preferred consistency. (Note that the hummus will thicken as it cools.) Season with salt as needed. Allow the hummus to cool to room temperature while you make the tostones.

To store: Refrigerate the hummus in an airtight container for up to 5 days. Stir before serving if any separation occurs.

Make the tostones: In a large bowl, dissolve the salt in the water. Add the plantain slices and submerge them in the water. Let them soak for 10 to 15 minutes—this will help prevent oxidation so the plantains don't turn brown. If the slices float, place a small plate or bowl on top to keep them submerged. Remove the plantains from the water and pat them dry with paper towels. They should be as dry as possible before frying so they don't splatter.

Set a medium frying pan over medium-high heat and add 2 to 3 inches of canola oil. Heat for about 5 minutes, until the temperature reaches 350°F. Add the plantain slices to the hot oil and fry them for 2 to 3 minutes, until lightly golden but not fully crisp. Remove them from the oil and drain on paper towels.

Using a plantain smasher, flatten each fried plantain slice to about ¼ inch thick. Return the flattened plantains to the hot oil and fry again for 1 to 2 minutes, or until crispy and golden brown. Remove and drain on fresh paper towels. Serve the tostones immediately, alongside the red bean hummus.

SOFRITO VERSUS SAZÓN

In Dominican cooking, the word *sazón* can cause confusion. Traditionally, *sazón criollo* refers to what many know as sofrito: a fragrant, fresh seasoning base made by blending onions, garlic, peppers, cilantro, culantro, and tomatoes. It's the foundation of countless dishes, from rice to stews.

By contrast, in U.S. supermarkets sazón is often sold as a dry seasoning packet, popularized by brands like Goya. This powdered blend—typically a mix of annatto, garlic, cumin, coriander, oregano, salt, and sometimes MSG—is not what Dominican cooks mean when they say sazón.

For our recipes, sofrito means the fresh, homemade seasoning base. If you want a shortcut, Loisa makes a high-quality jarred sofrito and also offers an organic, MSG-free dry sazón blend. Both are excellent stand-ins for cooking at home.

Afro-Cuban Mojo Olives with Peanuts

Makes about 2 cups

Olives hold a special place in Afro-Latino culture. They were introduced during Spanish colonization when imported European foods signified status and wealth. Over time, however, they became a staple to Puerto Rican, Dominican, and Cuban cooking, adding bold, briny flavor to dishes like empanadas, *asopao* (stew), *mofongo* (a mashed plantain dish), empanadas, and arroz con gandules.

This recipe (photograph on page 124) draws inspiration from Cuban mojo, a zesty marinade traditionally used in meats and seafood. Here, I use it to marinate olives instead. I also incorporate Afro-Cuban culinary influences, including warm allspice for depth and roasted peanuts for crunch. Bold and aromatic, this snack pairs beautifully with tropical cocktails.

¼ cup olive oil

4 garlic cloves, thinly sliced

1 small serrano or habanero chile, thinly sliced (use gloves to handle)

Zest and juice of 1 orange

1 tablespoon fresh lime juice

1 teaspoon ground cumin

1 teaspoon smoked paprika

½ teaspoon ground allspice

½ teaspoon kosher salt

2 cups mixed olives (such as manzanilla and gordal), rinsed and drained

¼ cup fresh cilantro, chopped

2 tablespoons roasted peanuts, chopped, for garnish

Make the mojo: Warm the olive oil in a small skillet or saucepan over medium-low heat, ensuring it stays below 200°F. Add the garlic and chile and cook for 1 to 2 minutes until fragrant but not browned. Remove the pan from the heat, then stir in the orange zest and juice, lime juice, cumin, smoked paprika, allspice, and salt. Let the mixture cool slightly, for 5 to 10 minutes.

In a medium bowl, combine the olives and cilantro. Pour the cooled mojo over the olives and gently toss to coat. For optimal flavor, marinate the olives at room temperature for at least 30 minutes. Garnish with roasted peanuts before serving.

Chef's Note: If making the the olives in advance, store them in an airtight container in the fridge for up to 2 days, and bring to room temperature before serving.

Pairing suggestion: Fair & Hotter (page 125)

Special equipment

Oil thermometer

Dominican Ahi Tiradito

Makes 6 to 8 servings

Tiradito is a dish of thinly sliced raw fish served sashimi-style and dressed with a citrus-based sauce just before serving, preserving the clean flavor and delicate texture of the fish. Though it traces its origins to Japanese-Peruvian cuisine, tiradito has been embraced across Latin America. In Mexico, it often takes on bold, spicy notes; my Dominican version uses a cured ahi tuna dressed with aguachile. The flavors draw from the DR's tropical and Creole influences, combining a spark of acidity with gentle heat, and regional fruit like mango, passionfruit, and sour orange.

Chef's Note: For the herb salad, use bright-tasting herbs like cilantro, mint, and flat-leaf parsley. Culantro (a relative of cilantro with a deeper, more pungent taste) can be added for an authentic Dominican touch. Avoid earthier herbs like basil, tarragon, or dill, which clash with the citrusy, peppery profile of the aguachile.

CURED AHI TUNA

3 tablespoons ground cumin

½ cup kosher salt

½ cup granulated sugar

2 tablespoons granulated garlic

1 pound ahi tuna, skin removed

AGUACHILE

4 ounces Chinola Passion Fruit Liqueur

1 cup fresh mango, peeled and diced

Zest and juice of 2 limes

½ Scotch bonnet pepper, seeded and sliced (use gloves to handle)

½ cup cilantro leaves, plus extra for garnish

2 tablespoons red miso

¼ cup sliced red onion

2 garlic cloves, smashed

FOR SERVING

½ cup pickled red onion, diced

½ cup herb salad (see Chef's Note)

½ cup pickled mango, finely diced

Tostones (page 127) or corn tortilla chips

Special equipment

Blender

Cure the tuna: In a small bowl, combine the cumin, salt, sugar, and granulated garlic—this is the curing mixture. Lay the tuna on a rimmed sheet pan and spread the curing mix over it, ensuring the tuna is completely covered. Cover with plastic wrap and place in the refrigerator to cure for 4 hours.

Make the aguachile: In a blender, combine the passion fruit liqueur, mango, lime juice and zest, Scotch bonnet pepper, cilantro, red miso, red onion, and garlic. Blend on low for 15 seconds, then on high for 1 minute until smooth. Transfer the mixture into a small container or bowl, cover, and refrigerate until ready to serve.

Make the tiradito: Remove the cured tuna from the refrigerator and rinse off the curing mixture with cold water. Pat dry with a paper towel, then place in the freezer for 10 to 15 minutes to ensure clean slices. Transfer the tuna to a cutting board and use a sharp knife to slice it against the grain into ⅛-inch-thick sashimi-style slices.

To serve: Spoon some aguachile into the bottom of each bowl or plate. Add a portion of the tuna, arranging the slices in overlapping layers. Garnish with pickled onion, herb salad, and pickled mango. Serve tostones or tortilla chips on the side.

Spicy (Picoso) Ají Amarillo Shrimp & Yuca Skewers

Makes 12 skewers

Grilled skewers—often served as pinchos—are popular in the Dominican Republic. They are a favorite at roadside stands, barbecues, and festivals, where they offer a quick, satisfying snack or meal. They're typically made with marinated meats and vegetables such as yuca, a starchy root vegetable with a slightly nutty texture. Here, hearty yuca is paired with juicy shrimp marinated in a paste made from ají amarillo, a fruity, spicy pepper beloved in Peruvian cooking.

12 large shrimp (16 to 20 count per pound), peeled and deveined

1 tablespoon fresh lime juice

½ teaspoon kosher salt (for shrimp marinade)

1 tablespoon ají amarillo paste (Peruvian yellow chile paste)

2 cloves garlic, finely minced

1 yuca root, peeled, cut into 1-inch cubes

1 tablespoon kosher salt (for boiling yuca)

Vegetable oil, for frying

1 tablespoon olive oil

2 tablespoons chopped fresh cilantro

If using wooden skewers, soak them in water for 20 to 30 minutes.

Prepare the shrimp: In a small, non-reactive bowl, marinate the shrimp by tossing them with the lime juice, salt, ají amarillo paste, and garlic. Let sit for 15 minutes while preparing the yuca. Do not marinate the shrimp for longer than 15 minutes.

Bring a medium pot with 2 quarts of water to a boil; then add 1 tablespoon of the salt. Add the yuca and simmer for 15 to 18 minutes, until the pieces are fork-tender but not falling apart. Drain well and pat completely dry.

Remove the shrimp from the marinade and pat dry.

In a large skillet, heat ¼ to ½ inch of vegetable oil over medium-high heat. Fry the yuca for 3 to 4 minutes, turning occasionally, until golden brown and crisp. Transfer to a plate lined with paper towels to drain excess oil. Carefully pour off the oil and wipe the skillet clean with a paper towel.

Return the skillet to medium heat and add 1 tablespoon fresh vegetable oil. Add the shrimp to the pan and sear for 1 to 1½ minutes per side, until opaque with a slight char. Remove from the heat.

Thread the shrimp and crispy yuca onto skewers, alternating the pieces. Sprinkle with cilantro and serve warm.

Special equipment

12 wooden or metal skewers

YUCA

Yuca is a key ingredient in Caribbean and Latin American cuisine with a fascinating transatlantic history. Native to South America, yuca was brought to West Africa during the transatlantic trade era, becoming a staple there. Over time, it also became deeply rooted in Caribbean cooking, completing a full-circle journey back across the Atlantic.

Today, the starchy root (also called cassava or manioc) is prized for its versatility and satisfying texture. It can be boiled, mashed, fried, or ground into flour and used in breads and fritters. When cooked properly, it has a creamy interior and a crisp exterior that holds up beautifully in both savory and sweet preparations. Always cook yuca before eating—raw yuca contains natural compounds that must be neutralized through soaking, boiling, or frying.

SALADO Y AHUMADO

SALTY & SMOKY

COCKTAILS

139 **Mark del Caribe**
Maker's Mark 46, coconut rum, plantain syrup, jerk bitters, hickory smoke

141 **Lake Breeze**
Mezcal, Sorel Liqueur, Cointreau, jerk bitters, lime

142 **Rooted in Oakland**
Mezcal, kiwi syrup, orange, falernum, habanero bitters, popping boba

145 **Mayaimi Swizzle**
coconut oil–washed Scotch, falernum, Demerara sugar, rose water, Angostura bitters, sour beer

146 **Over-the-Table Old Fashioned**
rye whiskey, spiced honey, mango nectar, falernum syrup, Angostura bitters

148 **El Premio**
Nixta Licor de Elote, tamarind-infused Mezcal, Amaro Montenegro, orange suya-spiced agave, clove bitters

BITES

149 **Cured Salmon Ceviche with Chinola Passion Fruit–Chile Marinade**

150 **Dungeness Crab–Stuffed Piquillo Peppers**

152 **Oysters with Afro-Dominican Cocktail Sauce & Mignonette**

153 **Afro-Dominican Roasted Chickpeas**

On Peated Scotch, Bourbon & Mezcal: The Smoky Spirits

The smoky flavors of peated Scotch, bourbon, and Mezcal come from distinct traditions; in Scotch, smoke comes from burning peat during malting. Bourbon picks up a caramelized flavor from aging in charred oak barrels, while Mezcal's smokiness comes from roasting agave hearts in ovens.

Smoky Scotch Whisky

Peat is formed over thousands of years from decomposing grass and moss. Once a common fuel source in Ireland and Scotland, it is used to heat barley during Scotch whisky production, the smoke imparting its flavor. Not all Scotch is peated or smoky—Scotch whiskies from the Lowlands and Speyside have little to no peat influence, offering lighter, malt-forward profiles. The intensity and character of a smoky Scotch depend on the peat type, terroir, and the length of exposure to the peat smoke during malting. Flavors range from earthy to floral, with hints of wood smoke, leather, or smoked meat. Peated Scotch is produced in Islay, an island off the west coast of Scotland known for its dense peat bogs and sea-salt air. Peated Scotch's character can range from subtle smoke to bold intensity, depending on region and technique.

Bourbon

While bourbon can be produced anywhere in the United States, it is most famously made in Kentucky, where the climate and limestone-filtered water contribute to its flavor. The region's dramatic seasonal temperature swings help the spirit expand and contract, moving into and out of the wood of barrels where it ages. By law, bourbon must be aged in new, charred oak barrels. Charring the barrels caramelizes the wood's natural sugars, creating flavors of caramel, toffee, and vanilla. The depth of these flavors depends on the char level:

Level 1 (15 seconds): Light caramelization for faster-aging whiskies.

Level 2 (30 seconds): Medium char for enhanced caramel notes.

Level 3 (35 seconds): Commonly used, producing rich, spicy flavors.

Level 4 (55 seconds): Known as "alligator char," it deeply cracks the wood, maximizing flavor extraction, perfect for bolder drinks like Mark del Caribe (page 139).

Mezcal

Derived from the Nahuatl word *Mexicali* (cooked agave), Mezcal is one of the world's smokiest spirits. *Piñas* (agave hearts) are roasted in underground ovens lined with volcanic rocks and agave (maguey) leaves, then smoked for several days to create earthy, chocolatey, and spicy notes. After roasting, the agave is crushed under a *tahona* (a massive volcanic stone wheel), fermented, and distilled.

Oaxaca, Mexico is the center of Mezcal production, where producers—like Graciela Ángeles Carreño of Real Minero—preserve traditional methods, such as clay-pot distillation and hand-harvesting of agave plants. Modern Mezcal is regulated under Norma Oficial Mexicana (NOM), which mandates that the spirit be made from 100 percent maguey. It defines three styles:

Mezcal: Made using ovens, mills, and modern methods.

Artisanal Mezcal: Roasted underground or in brick ovens, crushed by hand or stone, and distilled with *bagazo* (agave fibers).

Ancestral Mezcal: Produced using only traditional methods, including underground roasting and clay-pot distillation.

Mezcal is traditionally served in *copitas* (small clay cups) with orange slices and *sal de gusano* (worm salt), a salt with chiles and ground-up agave worms). The spirit's presence in cocktails is a recent development, but it makes a strong showing in this book, featured in drinks such as Last Conacado (page 101), My Familiar (page 118), Bidi Bidi Bom Bom (page 121), and Rooted in Oakland (page 142).

The Salty & Smoky Flavor Family

Smoke and salt give a cocktail (or dish) intensity and edge. From brine to char, this flavor family channels the elemental—bringing earth, ocean, and fire to the glass.

- bourbon
- brine
- charred wood
- hickory
- Mezcal
- peated Scotch
- sea salt
- smoked paprika
- smoke (from liquid smoke or a cocktail smoker)
- suya spice

FROM SAP TO SYRUP: UNDERSTANDING AGAVE

When I started experimenting behind the bar over a decade ago, agave was just "agave" in the U.S. Now, you can find raw, light, amber, dark amber, and even blue agave nectar varieties. So . . . what's the difference?

Raw agave, which is unheated, has a neutral flavor and is only lightly sweet. Light agave is minimally processed with a mild, slightly caramelized taste. Amber and dark agave develop rich caramel notes through cooking, with flavor intensity increasing as the syrup darkens. Blue agave nectar, made in Central Mexico exclusively from the *agave tequilana* (blue agave plant—the same plant used to make tequila). It's popular for its clean, mild taste.

Agave nectar is produced mainly in Jalisco from the plant's natural sap, *aguamiel* (honey water), which is sweeter and less viscous than honey. Each mature agave plant can yield up to six quarts of aguamiel daily, depending on species and growing conditions. Following traditional methods, farmers remove the plant's flower stalk, which allows aguamiel to collect in the central cavity before being siphoned out for processing—a technique largely unchanged since pre-Hispanic Mesoamerican civilizations.

Agave nectar plays a key part in this book's cocktails, as in the Dominican Date Sour (page 122), where its gentle, earthy sweetness lifts the tang of tamarind and lime. It plays an essential supporting role in mixology, supporting without overshadowing a drink's brighter or smokier elements.

Mark del Caribe

The name Mark del Caribe calls out both the drink's spirit—Maker's Mark bourbon—and its island soul, bridging the American South and the Caribbean. As for the cocktail, it's a bold fusion of Caribbean and Southern flavors, with bourbon as its backbone. Maker's Mark 46 provides rich, oaky depth that pairs beautifully with silky tropical coconut rum. Homemade Plantain Syrup offers a caramelized sweetness that balances out the spice of jerk bitters, while a hint of hickory lends smoky complexity inspired by fire-kissed flavors from the grill.

Chef's Note: If jerk bitters are unavailable, substitute 2 dashes Angostura bitters and 1 or 2 dashes of mild hot sauce (such as Crystal or Cholula).

1 ounce Maker's Mark 46 bourbon

1 ounce RumHaven coconut rum

¾ ounce Plantain Syrup (page 166)

2 dashes jerk bitters (see Chef's Note)

1 drop hickory liquid smoke, for finishing

Banana chip, for garnish

In a mixing glass, combine the Maker's Mark, coconut rum, Plantain Syrup, and jerk bitters with cubed ice. Stir vigorously for 20 to 30 seconds, until well chilled. Strain into a rocks glass over a large ice cube. Add a drop of hickory liquid smoke; then garnish with a banana chip and serve immediately.

Glassware

Rocks

Ice

1 cup cubed (for stirring)
plus 1 large cube (for serving)

Left

Lake Breeze

This cocktail draws inspiration from the "Red Drink," a cherished tradition in African American culture, especially during Juneteenth celebrations. Originating from West African hibiscus and kola nut beverages, the Red Drink represents the bloodshed of enslaved ancestors, symbolizes resilience. Microdistiller Jackie Summers' Sorel Liqueur—a modern interpretation of the Red Drink—adds its rich blend of hibiscus, clove, cinnamon, and nutmeg to the Lake Breeze.

The "Lake Breeze" name pays homage to Oakland's Lake Merritt, a central gathering place for Juneteenth festivities, where the community comes together to honor freedom and heritage. The addition of smoky Mezcal, bright citrus from Cointreau, and warming jerk bitters captures the spirit of these celebrations.

1 ounce Mezcal

¾ ounce Sorel Liqueur

½ ounce Cointreau (or good-quality triple sec of your choice)

2 dashes jerk bitters (see Chef's Note)

¾ ounce fresh lime juice

1 orange twist, for garnish (see page 156)

In a mixing glass, combine the Mezcal, Sorel Liqueur, Cointreau, jerk bitters, and lime juice with the ice. Stir until well chilled. Double strain into the glass over a large ice cube. Express an orange twist over the drink and drop it in as a garnish.

Spirit-Free Lake Breeze: Pre-chill the shaker and a rocks or coupe glass to minimize dilution. Replace the Mezcal with 1½ ounces Abstinence Cape Citrus and the Cointreau with ½ ounce Abstinence Epilogue X. Use Hibiscus Syrup (page 165) in place of the Sorel Liqueur. Substitute 2 dashes of All The Bitter Aromatic or New Orleans bitters for the jerk bitters. Shake with 1 cup cubed ice for 8 to 10 seconds, until the shaker is frosted and the drink is well chilled. Follow the main recipe to strain, garnish, and serve.

Pairing suggestion: Oysters with Afro-Dominican Cocktail Sauce and Mignonette (page 152)

Special equipment	Glassware	Ice
Fine-mesh cocktail strainer	Rocks or coupe	1 cup cubed (for shaking) plus 1 large cube (for serving)

Rooted in Oakland

I'll never forget the moment I stepped behind the bar for the first time at AlaMar on a packed First Friday in Oakland. What started as necessity—I was filling in for a missing bartender—turned out to be the spark that ignited a new passion. Learning to craft cocktails, much like cooking, was all about balance, storytelling, and honoring flavors that feel like home. Rooted in Oakland is one of the first cocktails I designed once I found my confidence behind the bar. It layers a base of smoky Mezcal with bright, tropical kiwi syrup and orange juice, habanero bitters to keep things interesting, and falernum syrup for a subtle thread of Caribbean spice.

1½ ounces Mezcal

¾ ounce kiwi syrup (like Monin or 1883 Maison Routin)

½ ounce fresh orange juice

¼ ounce falernum syrup

2 dashes habanero bitters

1 tablespoon lychee or mango popping boba, for garnish

1 orange twist, for garnish (see page 156)

In a shaker, combine the Mezcal, kiwi syrup, orange juice, falernum, and habanero bitters with cubed ice. Shake vigorously for 15 seconds, until the shaker is frosted on the outside and the drink is well chilled. Double strain into a rocks glass over a large ice cube. Spoon the popping boba over the drink. Express an orange twist over the top and drop it in as a garnish.

Chef's Note: Falernum, which originated in Barbados and is available as a syrup and a liqueur, is infused with lime zest, ginger, clove, and almond. It's a staple in island mixology, prized for adding layers of spice, citrus, and subtle nuttiness to cocktails. A splash of falernum instantly brings tropical drinks to life, infusing them with its distinctive bright spice and the spirit of the islands.

Pairing suggestion: Cured Salmon Ceviche with Chinola Passion Fruit–Chile Marinade (page 149)

Special equipment

Fine-mesh cocktail strainer

Glassware

Rocks

Ice

1 cup cubed ice (for shaking) plus 1 large cube (for serving)

Cured Salmon Ceviche with
Chinola Passion Fruit–Chile Marinade, page 149

Mayaimi Swizzle

This festive drink is named for the Indigenous Mayaimi people who once lived around the 730-square-mile Lake Mayaimi in present-day Florida ("mayaimi" means "big water"). Today, the lake is known as Lake Okeechobee, but this cocktail nods to Miami's ancestral roots. Bridging flavors from West Africa to the Caribbean to the Americas, it's built with a cross-cultural mix of coconut oil–washed Scotch, rose water, and spice-forward falernum liqueur. A float of sour beer on top is a direct reference to African fermented drinks like pito, umqombothi, and chibuku—ancestral brews made using spontaneous fermentation methods. Though not labeled "sour beers," they share the same funky, complex profile so beloved in craft brewing.

COCONUT OIL–WASHED SCOTCH

- 1 cup Scotch whisky
- 2 tablespoons melted coconut oil (refined for a lighter flavor or unrefined for a stronger flavor)

- 1½ ounces coconut oil–washed Scotch whisky
- ½ ounce falernum liqueur (or use falernum syrup and reduce Demerara Syrup to ¼ ounce)
- ½ ounce Demerara Syrup (page 165) (or ¼ ounce, if using falernum syrup)
- 3 dashes rose water
- 3 dashes Angostura bitters
- 2 ounces sour beer, to float (see page 20)
- Mint sprig, for garnish

Make the coconut oil–washed Scotch: In a nonreactive container, combine the whisky with melted coconut oil. Let sit at room temperature for 4 to 6 hours, stirring occasionally. Transfer to the freezer until the oil fully solidifies, at least 2 hours. Strain the Scotch through a fine-mesh strainer lined with cheesecloth to remove any solids. Store in the refrigerator and use within 2 weeks.

Make the cocktail: Fill a Collins glass with crushed ice. Add the coconut oil–washed Scotch, falernum liqueur, Demerara Syrup, rose water, and Angostura bitters. Using a swizzle stick or long-handled barspoon, swizzle vigorously for about 15 seconds, until the glass is frosty and the drink is well chilled. Top with additional crushed ice. Carefully float the sour beer over the cocktail by slowly pouring it into the glass over the back of a spoon, taking care to prevent mixing. Garnish with a mint sprig and serve immediately.

Chef's Note: The base of this drink can be batched and refrigerated for up to 3 days in advance. Batch without the sour beer; then add beer just before serving to preserve its effervescence. Do not freeze.

Special equipment	Glassware	Ice
Fine-mesh cocktail strainer	Collins glass	1 cup crushed (for mixing and serving)

Over-the-Table Old Fashioned

This is a Caribbean-inspired twist on the classic Old Fashioned, with warm island flavors bringing fresh kick to a timeless structure. It's the kind of cocktail that invites conversation and connection "over the table" and is meant to be shared and savored. The rich depth of Spiced Honey Syrup, combined with a splash of mango nectar, lends a tropical sweetness reminiscent of sun-ripened fruit. Falernum syrup adds subtle hints of clove, lime, and almond, and Angostura bitters, a signature of Caribbean cocktail culture, provide the finishing touch with bold spice and herbal complexity.

Chef's Note: Most commercial mango nectars contain added sugar, which balances tart ingredients in cocktails. If you're using an unsweetened version, you may want to adjust the recipe's sweetener.

2 ounces rye whiskey (such as Rittenhouse)

¼ ounce Spiced Honey Syrup (page 163)

¼ ounce mango nectar (see Chef's Note)

¼ ounce falernum syrup

3 dashes Angostura bitters

1 slice dried mango, for garnish

In a mixing glass, combine the rye whiskey, Spiced Honey Syrup, mango nectar, falernum syrup, and Angostura bitters with cubed ice. Stir vigorously for 20 to 30 seconds, until well chilled. Strain into a double rocks glass over a large ice cube. Garnish with dried mango and serve immediately.

Low-ABV Over-the-Table Old Fashioned: Pre-chill mixing glass and a double rocks glass to minimize dilution. Replace the rye whiskey with a nonalcoholic whiskey alternative, such as Lyre's American Malt or Spiritless Kentucky 74. Follow the rest of the recipe as written, but stir gently instead of vigorously.

Glassware

Double rocks

Ice

1 cup cubed (for stirring)
plus 1 large cube (for serving)

El Premio

This drink is called El Premio—"The Prize"—because it brings together treasured ingredients from two ancestral foodways: corn and Mezcal. Corn has been at the heart of Mesoamerican cuisine for thousands of years, and Nixta Licor de Elote, an ancestral corn liqueur from Jilotepec, Mexico, honors that heritage with deep, roasted sweetness and earthy complexity. Nixta's toasty notes meet the smoky tang of tamarind-infused Mezcal.

This cocktail also includes Orange Suya–Spiced Agave, a nod to the rich culinary traditions of West Africa. (*Suya,* a bold, nutty spice blend, is a cornerstone of West African street food culture.) The result is a drink that's bold, balanced, and deeply rooted in tradition.

¾ ounce Nixta Licor de Elote

1 ounce tamarind Mezcal (preferably El Silencio or see page 159)

1 ounce Amaro Montenegro

½ ounce Orange Suya–Spiced Agave (page 161)

2 dashes clove bitters

1 orange twist (see page 156), for garnish

In a mixing glass, combine the Nixta, tamarind-infused Mezcal, Amaro Montenegro, Orange Suya–Spiced Agave, and clove bitters with cubed ice. Stir vigorously for 20 to 30 seconds, until the mixing glass is frosted and the cocktail is well chilled. Strain into the glass over a large ice cube. Express an orange twist over the drink and drop it in as a garnish. Serve immediately.

Low-ABV El Premio: Pre-chill the mixing glass and rocks glass to minimize dilution. Replace the tamarind-infused Mezcal with 1 ounce Abstinence Epilogue X plus ½ ounce tamarind paste purée, adjusting for sweetness as needed. Reduce the Amaro Montenegro (23% ABV) to ¼ ounce and the Nixta Licor de Elote (30% ABV) to ½ ounce. Follow the instructions in the main recipe to combine. Stir gently for 20 to 30 seconds, until the mixing glass is frosted, and the cocktail is well chilled. Strain and garnish as above.

Pairing suggestion: Afro-Dominican Roasted Chickpeas (page 153)

Glassware

Rocks

Ice

1 cup cubed (for stirring)
plus 1 large cube (for serving)

Cured Salmon Ceviche with Chinola Passion Fruit–Chile Marinade

Makes 6 servings

Wild salmon, first cured with a cumin-forward blend is then combined with a bright and aromatic passion fruit–chile marinade (photograph on page 143). The marinade, inspired by the bold flavors of aguachile, blends fresh lime juice, Chinola Passion Fruit Liqueur, pineapple, Fresno chile, and herbs for a tangy, slightly spicy balance. Served with crispy tostones, this dish combines richness, acidity, and crunch for a refreshing bite.

CURED SALMON

- 1 pound wild salmon
- 3 tablespoons ground cumin
- ½ cup kosher salt
- ½ cup sugar
- 2 tablespoons garlic powder

PASSION FRUIT–CHILE MARINADE

Makes 2 to 2¼ cups

- 1 cup Chinola Passion Fruit Liqueur
- 1 cup diced pineapple
- Zest and juice of 2 limes
- ½ Fresno chile, sliced
- ½ cup cilantro leaves
- ¼ cup mint leaves
- ¼ cup chopped red onion
- 2 cloves garlic, smashed

CEVICHE

- ½ cup diced red onion
- 2 Fresno chiles, deseeded and diced
- 2 red radishes, thinly sliced, for garnish
- Cilantro sprigs, for garnish
- Tostones, for serving (page 127)

Cure the salmon: In a medium bowl, combine the cumin, salt, sugar, and garlic powder—this is the curing mixture. Place the salmon on a rimmed sheet pan. Coat the salmon evenly with the curing mixture, ensuring complete coverage. Cover and refrigerate for 4 hours.

Make the passion fruit–chile marinade: In a blender, combine the passion fruit liqueur, pineapple, lime zest and juice, chile, cilantro, mint, red onion, and garlic. Blend on low speed for 15 seconds, until the ingredients start to break down, then increase to high speed and blend for about 1 minute, until very smooth and lightly frothy. Transfer to a bowl, cover, and refrigerate until ready to use. This can be made up to 3 days in advance. Stir before using.

Prepare the ceviche: Remove the salmon from the refrigerator and rinse off the curing mixture with cold water. Pat the salmon dry with paper towels. Dice the salmon into ¼-inch cubes and transfer to a large bowl. Add the red onion, chiles, and ¼ cup of the passion fruit–chile marinade. Toss gently to coat.

To serve: Spread a layer of passion fruit–chile marinade on the bottom of a shallow serving bowl (8 to 10 inches wide). Arrange the ceviche on one side of the bowl in a half-moon shape. Garnish with sliced radish and fresh cilantro sprigs. Enjoy immediately, served with tostones.

Pairing Suggestion: Rooted in Oakland (page 142)

Special equipment

Blender

Dungeness Crab–Stuffed Piquillo Peppers

Makes 4 servings

These stuffed peppers are the perfect small bite: sweet Dungeness crab and savory oyster mushrooms cooked in a zesty salsa criolla, stuffed into sweet piquillo peppers and layered with the creamy, richness of queso amarillo. You can find Dominican queso amarillo at many Latin American grocery stores or online from specialty shops—search for "queso Amarillo Dominicano."

Chef's Note: If grilled jarred piquillo peppers are unavailable, substitute jarred Peppadew sweet piquanté peppers. They're smaller, so you'll need 16 to 20 of them.

SALSA CRIOLLA

Makes about 1 cup

- 1 tablespoon vegetable oil
- 1 cup diced red and green bell peppers
- ¼ cup finely chopped yellow onion
- 3 cloves garlic, thinly sliced
- ¼ cup dry white wine
- 2 tablespoons Spanish green olives, thinly sliced
- 1 tablespoon Dominican sazón (preferably Loisa brand)
- 2 tablespoons tomato paste
- ½ cup crab or seafood stock

CRAB FILLING

- 3 tablespoons vegetable oil
- 1½ cups shredded or sliced oyster mushrooms
- 1 cup diced Peppadew sweet piquanté peppers
- 3 ounces cooked Dungeness crab or lobster meat
- 1 cup Salsa Criolla
- ½ cup cilantro, finely chopped

FOR ASSEMBLY

- 8 jarred whole grilled piquillo peppers, patted dry (from 1 or 2 jars, depending on size)
- ½ cup shredded Dominican queso amarillo
- ¼ cup shaved Dominican queso amarillo, for serving

Make the salsa criolla: In a medium saucepan, heat the vegetable oil over medium heat. Sauté the bell peppers, onion, and garlic for 4 to 5 minutes, until tender. Deglaze with white wine, scraping the pan to release any browned bits. Add the olives, sazón, and tomato paste and stir to incorporate. Add crab stock and simmer for 8 to 10 minutes, until reduced by about one-third and the consistency is lightly saucy. Continue simmering, stirring occasionally, until the salsa is glossy, 2 to 3 minutes longer. Let cool before using. The salsa criolla can be made ahead and refrigerated in an airtight container for up to 3 days.

Make the crab filling: Set a small sauté pan over medium heat and add the vegetable oil. Once the oil is hot, add the mushrooms and sauté for 3 to 4 minutes, until golden. Add the Peppadew peppers and sauté for 30 seconds, until they are slightly softened. Add the crab meat and stir to evenly distribute, breaking up any larger pieces. Cook for 1 to 2 minutes, until the mixture is heated through. Stir in the salsa criolla and cook until the mixture is thick enough to hold its shape when spooned and no liquid pools at the bottom of the pan, 2 to 3 minutes. Remove from the heat and fold in the cilantro.

Stuff and bake the piquillo peppers: Preheat the oven to 375°F and line a baking sheet with parchment paper. Fill each piquillo pepper with 2 to 3 tablespoons of the crab mixture depending on size, and top with 1 tablespoon of shredded queso amarillo. Arrange the peppers on the baking sheet and bake for 8 to 10 minutes, until the mixture is bubbling. Top with the queso amarillo and serve hot.

Pairing suggestion: Tropical Noir (page 91)

Oysters with Afro-Dominican Cocktail Sauce & Mignonette

Makes 4 to 6 servings

This dish is my Afro-Dominican spin on a classic raw oyster dish. Here, the oysters' natural brininess pairs perfectly with a bold, tangy, tamarind-forward cocktail sauce and bright, spicy, and refreshing mignonette. The Afro-Dominican cocktail sauce features tamarind (native to Africa) for tartness, and culantro (a staple in Dominican cooking) for fresh, herbal brightness. The mignonette is spiked with sofrito for a distinctive Caribbean touch and includes serrano peppers for a bit of heat.

AFRO-DOMINICAN COCKTAIL SAUCE

Makes 1¼ cups

- 1 cup ketchup
- ½ teaspoon Tabasco, or other vinegar-based hot sauce, to taste
- 1 tablespoon tamarind paste mixed with 3 tablespoons warm water, stirred until smooth (use 2 to 4 tablespoons of this mixture, to taste)
- Zest and juice of 1 lemon
- 2 tablespoons freshly grated horseradish
- 1 tablespoon finely chopped culantro or cilantro
- Kosher salt
- Black pepper

SPICY MIGNONETTE

Makes 1½ cups

- 1 cup apple cider vinegar
- ½ large red onion, finely chopped
- 2 tablespoons sofrito
- 1 teaspoon chopped pickled ginger
- 1 apple, peeled, cored, and finely diced
- ¼ bunch cilantro, finely chopped
- ½ serrano chile, finely minced
- Black pepper

OYSTERS

- 24 fresh oysters, shucked
- 4 to 6 cups crushed ice, for serving
- Lemon wedges or herb sprigs, for serving

Place a platter large enough to hold the oysters in the refrigerator to chill while you prepare the sauce and mignonette.

Make the cocktail sauce: In a medium bowl, whisk together the ketchup, Tabasco, 2 tablespoons of tamarind juice, the lemon zest and juice, horseradish, and culantro until smooth. Season with salt and pepper, and add additional tamarind juice to taste. Transfer to a clean serving bowl and set aside.

Make the mignonette: In a medium bowl, combine the vinegar, onion, sofrito, pickled ginger, apple, cilantro, and serrano. Stir gently to combine. Transfer the mignonette to a clean serving bowl and set aside. The cocktail sauce and mignonette can be made up to 3 days in advance. Store each in a separate airtight container in the refrigerator. Stir before serving.

To serve: Spread the crushed ice on the chilled platter. Arrange the freshly shucked oysters on the platter on top of the ice. Garnish the platter with lemon wedges or a few sprigs of fresh herbs. Serve the cocktail sauce and mignonette alongside.

Pairing Suggestion: Lake Breeze (page 141)

Afro-Dominican Roasted Chickpeas

Makes about 2 cups

Chickpeas, or garbanzo beans, have long been a staple in both West African and Dominican kitchens. They were introduced to the island through Spanish colonization, but have since been embraced and reimagined with Afro-Caribbean influences. This snack takes inspiration from the bold, smoky, and herbaceous seasonings found in Dominican sazón (or sofrito), blending smoked paprika, culantro, Dominican oregano, and spicy Scotch bonnet peppers for a crunchy, addictive bite.

Chef's Note: Dominican oregano, also known as oregano de la isla, has a bolder, earthier flavor than Mediterranean oregano. If unavailable, you can use Mediterranean oregano, but double the amount for a closer match.

1 teaspoon kosher salt

1 teaspoon smoked paprika

½ teaspoon ground cumin

½ teaspoon dried Dominican oregano

¼ teaspoon ground Scotch bonnet powder (or cayenne pepper)

1 (15-ounce) can chickpeas, rinsed and drained

2 tablespoons olive oil

Zest of 1 sour orange (or equal parts orange and lime zest)

2 tablespoons chopped fresh culantro or cilantro

Preheat the oven to 400°F. Line a baking sheet with parchment paper.

First, make the seasoning mixture: In a small bowl, combine the salt, smoked paprika, cumin, oregano, and Scotch bonnet powder. Set aside.

Pat the chickpeas as dry as possible to remove any remaining moisture. (This helps them crisp up rather than steam in the oven.) Spread the chickpeas in a single layer on the prepared baking sheet, drizzle with the olive oil, and toss until evenly coated.

Roast for 20 to 30 minutes. At the 10-minute mark, give the pan a shake to redistribute the chickpeas. Check on them at the 20-minute mark, and if they still seem soft, roast for an additional 5 to 10 minutes. They should be golden brown, slightly blistered, and feel crunchy to the touch. Remove the chickpeas from the oven, and while still hot, sprinkle them with the seasoning mixture. Toss to coat and let cool slightly, about 10 minutes.

Transfer the chickpeas to a bowl, add the citrus zest and culantro, and toss to incorporate. Serve warm or at room temperature. Store in an airtight container for up to 3 days. If the chickpeas lose crispness, you can toast them in the oven at 350°F for 5 minutes.

ACARDI

FROM SCRATCH: GARNISHES, INFUSIONS, SYRUPS & MILKS

The magic of a great cocktail often lies in the details—the homemade garnishes, infusions, syrups, and milks that transform a good drink into an unforgettable one. This section gathers these essential elements, giving you everything you need to create well-rounded flavor experiences.

Garnishes

Garnishes in this book are used to enhance aroma, texture, and flavor, not just visual appeal. They are selected to complement the specific ingredients in each cocktail, creating a complete sensory experience.

Candied yam slices: Cut a yam into ¼-inch rounds, toss them with ½ cup simple syrup (see page 20), and bake at 300°F for 30 to 45 minutes, flipping once halfway through, until golden. Cool before using. Store in an airtight container at room temperature for up to 3 days. For best texture, allow to dry fully before storing.

Cocktail cherries: Cocktail cherries come in several styles, each adding its own character to drinks. **Brandied cherries** are preserved in brandy, sugar, and sometimes spices, offering a rich, sweet, slightly boozy flavor. **Amarena or Luxardo Maraschino cherries**, small tart Italian cherries preserved in syrup, are another premium option. Though not brandied, their deep color and complex, fruity sweetness make them a favorite garnish in elevated cocktails.

Dehydrated orange, lemon, or lime wheels: Slice citrus into rounds approximately ⅛ to ¼ inch thick. Arrange them on a parchment-lined baking sheet and bake at 200°F for 2 to 3 hours, flipping halfway through, until fully dried but still vibrant in color. **For a chile-infused variation:** Sprinkle the slices with equal parts ground ancho chile powder, cayenne, and sugar before baking. To store, transfer the cooled citrus wheels to an airtight container and keep in a cool, dry place for up to 1 month.

Guava-dipped marshmallows: Combine ½ cup guava paste with 2 tablespoons water in a small saucepan. Set over low heat and cook, stirring frequently, for 5 to 7 minutes, until the guava paste dissolves and the mixture is thick, smooth, and glossy. Allow the guava mixture to cool slightly before dipping the marshmallows. Dip the marshmallows halfway, let excess drip off, and set on parchment paper to dry for 15 to 20 minutes. This amount coats 12 to 16 standard-size marshmallows. Store in a single layer in an airtight container at cool room temperature for up to 2 days. Used in Doña Rosa (page 105) and Santa Rosa (page 36).

Orange twist (or any citrus twist): Wash the fruit thoroughly. Use a vegetable peeler to peel a long, thin strip of peel (about ½ inch wide and 2 to 4 inches long), avoiding as much pith as possible. To use, hold the peel over the cocktail and gently twist it between your fingers to release the aromatic oils from its skin onto the surface of the drink; this is called expressing. You can also rub the drink around the rim of the glass. To make a spiral garnish, cut a longer strip of peel; then wrap the peel tightly around a straw, skewer, or barspoon. Hold it there for 5 to 10 seconds so it takes shape; then remove and place it on the drink. **For a burnt or toasted citrus peel:** For a more intense, aromatic garnish, use a strip of lemon or orange peel (2 to 3 inches long). Hold it with tongs or tweezers and gently toast the peel over an open flame—such as a gas burner or kitchen torch—until the edges darken and the oils begin to release. Express the warm peel over the drink and drop it in as a garnish, or discard after expressing for a subtle smoky citrus aroma. Always toast just before serving.

Infused Spirits

Infused spirits allow you to create custom flavors by combining a base spirit with various ingredients. Infusions take time—often a few days—so if you want to use these in a recipe, plan ahead!

Ancho Chile–Infused Mezcal

Makes about 750 mL

Used in Last Conacado (page 101) and My Familiar (page 118).

750 mL Mezcal

2 dried ancho chiles

Discard the stems and tear the ancho chiles into 3 or 4 pieces each to expose more surface area. Combine the chiles and Mezcal in a clean, sealable glass jar. Seal tightly and shake to mix. Store in a cool, dark place for 12 to 24 hours, tasting periodically for flavor.

Once the desired flavor is achieved, strain the Mezcal through a fine-mesh cocktail strainer or cheesecloth into a sterilized bottle, discarding the solids. Label with the date and ingredients. The infusion will last indefinitely at room temperature, but for best flavor, use within 3 to 6 months.

Chef's Note: For a deeper, roasted flavor, lightly toast the ancho chiles in a dry skillet over medium heat for 30 seconds per side before infusing. For a spicier kick, add ½ of a dried chipotle or guajillo chile to the infusion.

Special equipment

Fine-mesh cocktail strainer or cheesecloth

Clove-Infused Spiced Rum

Makes about 750 mL

Used in Santa Rosa (page 36), "Chocolate de Maní" Cocktail (page 95), and Captain's Final Word (page 66).

6 to 8 whole cloves

750 mL high-quality dark rum (such as Bumbu or Planteray Original Dark)

In a clean, sealable jar, combine the cloves and rum. Seal and let infuse in a cool, dark place for 24 to 48 hours, tasting periodically for flavor.

Once the desired flavor is achieved, strain through a fine-mesh cocktail strainer or cheesecloth into a sterilized bottle, discarding the cloves. Store at room temperature, labeled with the preparation date and ingredients. For best flavor, use within 3 to 6 months.

Special equipment

Fine-mesh strainer or cheesecloth

Chef's Note: **For a rounder spice profile, add one crushed allspice berry or a strip of dried orange peel.**

Tamarind-Infused Mezcal

Makes about 750 mL

Used in El Premio (page 148).

3½ ounces (¼ cup plus 3 tablespoons) tamarind paste purée

¾ cup water

¼ cup sugar (or to taste)

750 mL Mezcal or whiskey

In a small saucepan set over medium heat, mix together the tamarind paste and water, stirring gently until smooth. Add the sugar and stir until dissolved. Remove from heat and cool to room temperature.

Combine the cooled tamarind mixture with the Mezcal in a clean, sealable glass jar. Seal tightly, shake to mix, and store in a cool, dark place for 3 to 5 days, shaking gently once daily to prevent separation.

After 3 to 5 days, strain the infused spirit through a fine-mesh strainer or cheesecloth into a sterilized bottle. Label with the preparation date and ingredients. The infusion will last indefinitely at room temperature, but for best flavor, use within 3 to 6 months.

Special equipment

Fine-mesh strainer or cheesecloth

Chef's Note: Adjust sugar levels to your preferred sweetness, or experiment with spices like cinnamon or clove for added depth.

Infused Honey & Agave

Infused honey and agave syrups bring layered flavor, warmth, and subtle spice to several cocktails throughout this book, adding complexity without overwhelming the base spirits. Whether you're using honey or agave as the base, adjust the proportions of flavoring agents according to your preference. Infused honey is best prepared only to slightly warm, as excessive heat may diminish its natural qualities.

Yerba Maté Spiced Honey

Makes approximately 1 cup

Used in Chan Chan (page 44) and Fair & Hotter (page 125).

¼ cup loose yerba maté tea leaves

1 cinnamon stick

½ teaspoon ground cardamom

1 cup honey

Special equipment

Fine-mesh strainer

In a small saucepan over low heat, combine the yerba maté, cinnamon stick, cardamom, and honey. Stir gently until the honey warms and the flavors infuse, about 5 minutes; do not let it boil.

Remove from the heat and allow the mixture to cool to room temperature. Strain the honey through a fine-mesh strainer into a sterilized container, discarding the solids. Store the honey for up to 2 weeks in an airtight jar at room temperature or in the refrigerator.

Orange Suya-Spiced Agave

Makes about ½ cup

Used in Dominican Date Sour (page 122), Fair & Hotter (page 125), and El Premio (page 148).

- **¼ cup agave nectar**
- **¼ cup fresh orange juice**
- **½ teaspoon ground ginger**
- **¼ teaspoon smoked paprika**
- **½ teaspoon cayenne pepper**
- **¼ teaspoon ground toasted peanuts**
- **Pinch of kosher salt**

Special equipment

Fine-mesh strainer

In a small saucepan set over low heat, combine the agave nectar and orange juice. Stir in the ground ginger, smoked paprika, cayenne, ground toasted peanuts, and salt. Heat gently, stirring often, until the mixture is fully combined and aromatic, about 2 minutes. Remove from the heat and cool slightly, for 5 to 10 minutes. Strain through a fine-mesh strainer into a clean container, discarding the solids. Store in an airtight container in the refrigerator for up to 1 week.

Syrups

Syrups in this book are used to layer flavor, balance sweetness, and add depth to cocktails. Each syrup recipe I've included is tailored to highlight the unique ingredients and traditions behind the drinks.

Banana Syrup

Makes about 1 cup

Used in La Loma (page 33), Chan Chan (page 44), and Valdez Punch (page 69).

1 cup ripe mashed banana (about 2 bananas)

1 cup sugar

½ cup water

¼ teaspoon vanilla extract

Special equipment

Fine-mesh strainer

In a small saucepan set over medium heat, combine the mashed banana, sugar, and water. Stir until the sugar dissolves and the mixture begins to simmer, 3 to 5 minutes. Reduce the heat to low and simmer gently for 5 minutes, stirring occasionally, until slightly thickened and glossy. Remove from the heat and cool slightly, 5 to 10 minutes. Strain through a fine-mesh sieve into a clean container, pressing gently to extract liquid without pushing any solids through. Stir in the vanilla extract. Store in an airtight container in the refrigerator for up to 2 weeks.

Spiced Honey Syrup

Makes approximately 1 cup

Used in La Lucia (optional, page 46), "Chocolate de Maní" Cocktail (page 95), Cafecito de la Mesa (page 103), Over-the-Table Old Fashioned (page 146), and Yaniqueques (optional, page 57).

¼ cup warm water
1 cinnamon stick
1 teaspoon whole allspice berries
1 teaspoon grated fresh ginger
1 cup honey

Special equipment

Fine-mesh cocktail strainer

In a small saucepan over low heat, combine the water, cinnamon stick, allspice, ginger, and honey. Stir gently until the honey warms and the flavors infuse, about 5 minutes; do not let it boil. Remove from the heat and cool slightly, 15 to 20 minutes. Strain through a fine-mesh strainer into a sterilized container, discarding the solids. Store for up to 2 weeks in an airtight jar at room temperature or in the refrigerator.

Candied Yam Syrup

Makes about 1½ cups

Used in Candied Culture (page 35), La Cultura Old Fashioned (page 93), Doña Rosa (page 105), and Yaniquques (optional, page 57).

- **2 medium-small American orange-fleshed yams (sweet potatoes) peeled and cut into 1-inch chunks (about 2½ cups)**
- **1 cup sugar**
- **¾ cup water**
- **½ teaspoon ground cinnamon**
- **¼ teaspoon ground nutmeg**
- **¼ teaspoon ground ginger**
- **Pinch of kosher salt**
- **1 teaspoon vanilla extract**

Special equipment

Blender, fine-mesh strainer

Preheat the oven to 375°F. Spread the yams in a single layer on a parchment-lined baking sheet. Roast until deeply caramelized and fork-tender, 25 to 30 minutes, flipping halfway through.

In a medium saucepan, combine the roasted yams with the sugar, water, cinnamon, nutmeg, ginger, and salt. Bring to a simmer over medium heat, stirring to dissolve the sugar. Reduce the heat to low and cook until the yams break down (they should mash easily when pressed) and the syrup thickens enough to lightly coat the back of a spoon, about 15 minutes.

Remove from the heat and stir in the vanilla extract. Let the mixture cool for 10 to 15 minutes, then transfer to a blender and purée until smooth. Strain through a fine-mesh sieve into a clean container, pressing to extract as much syrup as possible. Discard the solids. If you want a thinner syrup, add water a teaspoon at a time until the mixture reaches your desired consistency. Store in an airtight container in the refrigerator for up to 1 week.

Demerara Syrup

Makes about 1 cup

½ cup Demerara sugar

½ cup water

In a small saucepan over low heat, combine the sugar and water. Stir gently until the sugar has fully dissolved and the syrup is clear, 3 to 5 minutes. Remove from heat and let cool to room temperature, 15 to 20 minutes. Transfer to a sterilized glass container and store in the refrigerator for up to 1 month. If it thickens too much, let it come to room temperature or gently rewarm the syrup before using.

Hibiscus Syrup (Sorrel Syrup)

Makes about 1½ cups

Used in Spirit-Free Santa Rosa (page 36), To Die Dreaming (page 41), Spirit-Free Bon Swa (page 72), The Latinidad Is Libre (page 88), and Lake Breeze (page 141).

1 cup prepared Sorrel (page 48)

1 cup sugar

Special equipment

Fine-mesh strainer

In a small saucepan set over medium heat, combine the prepared sorrel and sugar. Stir until the sugar fully dissolves, then bring to a gentle simmer. Reduce the heat to low and simmer gently for 5 minutes—it should be fragrant. Remove from the heat and strain through a fine-mesh sieve into a clean container, discarding the solids. Cool completely; then store in an airtight container in the refrigerator for up to 2 weeks.

Chef's Note: For a syrup that's less sweet, use ¾ cup sugar instead of 1 cup. Adjust sweetness to taste when using in cocktails. If you don't have sorrel, you can substitute strong hibiscus tea (steeped double-strength). Add ginger, clove, and cinnamon during simmering if you'd like a closer flavor match.

Plantain Syrup

Makes about 1 cup

Used in Tropical Noir (page 91), Moka on the Table (page 99), and Mark del Caribe (page 139).

1 ripe plantain, peeled and sliced
1 cup water
1 cup sugar
½ teaspoon kosher salt

Special equipment

Fine-mesh strainer

In a small saucepan set over medium heat, combine the plantain, water, sugar, and salt. Stir until the sugar dissolves and the mixture reaches a simmer. Reduce the heat to low and cook for 10 to 15 minutes, Stir the mixture occasionally while simmering to prevent sticking or scorching, until the plantain is very soft and easily mashed with the back of a spoon. Remove from the heat and let cool until it is warm but no longer steaming, about 10 minutes. Strain through a fine-mesh sieve into a clean container, pressing on the solids to extract as much liquid as possible. Discard the solids. Store the syrup in an airtight container in the refrigerator for up to 1 week.

Guajillo Chile Agave Syrup

Makes about 1 cup

Used in Spice Me Down (page 117) and My Familiar (page 118).

½ cup agave nectar

½ cup water

1 dried guajillo chile, stemmed and seeded

Special equipment

Fine-mesh strainer

Tear the guajillo chile into smaller pieces to increase surface area. In a small saucepan set over low heat, combine the agave nectar, water, and chile. Stir to combine, then cook, stirring often, until aromatic, about 5 minutes. Remove from the heat and cool slightly, 10 to 15 minutes. Strain through a fine-mesh sieve into a clean container, discarding the solids. Store in an airtight container in the refrigerator for up to 1 week.

Spicy Guava Syrup

Makes about 1 cup

Used in Valdez Punch (page 69).

½ cup guava paste
½ cup water
½ cup sugar
½ teaspoon ground cinnamon
3 whole cloves
⅛ teaspoon cayenne pepper

Special equipment

Fine-mesh strainer

In a small saucepan set over medium heat, combine the guava paste, water, sugar, cinnamon, cloves, and cayenne. Stir until the sugar and guava paste are fully dissolved. Once the mixture reaches a simmer, adjust the heat to low and cook for 5 minutes, stirring occasionally, to allow the spices and cayenne to infuse into the mixture. Remove from heat and let cool to room temperature. Strain through a fine-mesh strainer into a clean container, discarding the solids. Store in an airtight container in the refrigerator for up to 2 weeks.

Milks

We use a variety of milks in this book to add creaminess to the drinks. You can read more about them on page 96. One of these, the corn–coconut milk (recipe below) can't be store-bought but is well worth the effort!

Corn Coconut Milk FROM ALEKA ROSS

Makes about 3½ cups

Used in La Loma (page 33), Gingerbread Holiday Milk Punch (page 51), and Gracias Ancestros (page 74).

6 ears organic fresh corn, shucked

¼ cup water

¾ cup unsweetened coconut cream

Special equipment

Blender, fine-mesh strainer, cheesecloth

Fill a large pot with water and bring to a boil over high heat. Add the corn and cook until tender, about 10 minutes. Remove the corn from the water and let cool (you can discard the water).

Once the corn is cool enough to handle, use a sharp knife to cut the kernels off the cobs. Transfer them to a blender and add ¼ cup water. Blend until smooth. Strain the mixture through a fine-mesh strainer into a clean container, pressing down with a spatula or spoon to extract liquid without pushing solids through. Strain again through cheesecloth, squeezing to extract as much liquid as possible. Discard the solids.

Add the coconut cream to the corn liquid and stir until fully incorporated. Use immediately, or refrigerate in an airtight container for up to 3 days. Shake just before use, as separation may occur.

ACKNOWLEDGMENTS

Nelson German

A huge thank-you to Nikki Ballere Callnan at NBC Pottery for creating special ceramics to show off my culinary creations.

To my incredible family—thank you for always being my foundation and for surrounding me with love through every season of this journey.

To my beautiful wife, May German—your patience, strength, and belief in me have been my anchor. Thank you for standing by me, lifting me up, and keeping me grounded with your love.

To my friends, thank you for pushing me when I wanted to give up, for reminding me of my purpose, and for keeping me inspired.

To every colleague I've worked alongside over the years—thank you for the knowledge shared, the lessons learned, and the moments that shaped me.

To all my chef friends and my *Top Chef* family—your drive, creativity, and authenticity continue to push me to grow and evolve. I'm proud to be in this community with you.

To Andréa Lawson Gray—thank you for your incredible partnership, for helping me bring my voice to life on the page, and for believing in the soul of this book from day one.

And to Claire Yee and the entire Ten Speed Press team—thank you for helping make a dream come true. Your support, vision, and dedication turned this passion project into something real, lasting, and meaningful. I will honor you always.

To my ancestors—your sacrifices made my path possible. I honor you with every step I take and every dish and cocktail I create.

And to all the amazing bartenders—thank you for your creativity, your energy, and your artistry. Your influence runs through these pages.

Andréa Lawson Gray

First and always I want to thank my three amazing children, Andre, Armand, and Cienna Gray, for believing in me, encouraging me, and listening to me rant. Your unwavering support means everything to me.

To Nelson German, thank you for trusting me with your story. It is an incredible honor to share your journey.

To Aldana Iturri, whose diligence, attention to detail, and endless patience in testing and retesting recipes were invaluable.

To our editor, Claire Yee, thank you for your insight and guidance—for seeing the potential in this project and helping to shape it with such care.

To Nikki Ballere Callnan at NBC Pottery, whose beautiful ceramics elevate our visual storytelling—thank you for your craft and care.

To Betsy Stromberg, our designer, who immediately understood the spirit of the book and brought it to life.

To Eduardo (Eddie) Gonzalez, our photographer—mil gracias for your dedication, talent, and diligence.

To Fanesha Fabre, whose watercolors add depth and beauty to these pages—thank you for lending your artistry.

To Allie Kiekhofer, our copy editor—your keen eye and thoughtful edits made this a better book.

To Lauren MacLeod, thank you for believing in this book from the very beginning and championing it every step of the way.

To Tanya Holland, thank you for your steady support and confidence in my work. You are the seed from which this book sprouted.

ABOUT THE CONTRIBUTORS

Nelson German is a celebrated Afro-Latino chef, restaurateur, and culinary innovator known for his bold, culturally driven cuisine. He is the owner and executive chef of AlaMar Dominican Kitchen, the only Dominican restaurant on the West Coast, and Sobre Mesa, a vibrant Afro-Latino cocktail lounge, both located in Oakland, California. He recently expanded his culinary reach with the opening of Meski, a collaboration with Guma Aguiar and Golden State Warriors' Draymond Green, further solidifying his role as a leader in the culinary world.

A *Top Chef* alum, Nelson's work is deeply influenced by his Dominican heritage and African roots, blending the rich, layered flavors of the Caribbean with modern techniques and global influences. His cooking has earned national recognition for its creativity and cultural depth, making him one of the most influential voices in contemporary American cuisine.

In addition to his culinary skills, Nelson's creativity behind the bar has earned him the respect of mixology veterans. He is known for crafting inventive, flavor-forward cocktails that draw on the same cultural roots that define his cooking.

Nelson is a passionate advocate for diversity and inclusion in the culinary industry at large. He mentors young chefs, supports community initiatives, and champions Afro-Latino cuisine on the national stage, turning his restaurants into cultural hubs that celebrate the resilience, creativity, and innovation of the diaspora.

Andréa Lawson Gray is a food writer, food historian, and chef, and the co-author of the James Beard Award–winning *Convivir: Modern Mexican Cooking in California's Wine Country* (Rogelio Garcia, Abrams, September 2024). She is also the co-author of *Celebraciones Mexicanas: History, Recipes & Traditions.*

Her work blends cultural history and culinary storytelling, reflecting a deep appreciation for the intersections of food, migration, and identity. As a private chef, Andréa creates elevated dining experiences that highlight the rich, layered flavors of the global kitchen, drawing on influences from the Caribbean, Mexico, and beyond.

Andréa lives in San Francisco and New York City, where she continues to explore the connections between food, culture, and community.

Eduardo Gonzalez is a Bay Area photographer and co-founder of LemonAd Media, a production company specializing in food and beverage photography. He discovered his passion for cocktails while bartending at Trader Vic's in Emeryville and later refined his eye for storytelling while studying documentary filmmaking in London. Today, he helps restaurants captivate their audiences with clean, intentional imagery that reflects his precise, quietly artistic style.

Fanesha Fabre is a multidisciplinary illustrator whose work celebrates her lived experience as a Latina in New York City. Through bold, vibrant illustrations, she captures the textures, stories, and rhythms of her everyday surroundings—transforming the familiar into elevated visual narratives rooted in culture and authenticity.

INDEX BY ALCOHOL

Note: Page numbers in *italics* indicate photographs.

Specialty Spirits

TEN SPEED PRESS
An imprint of the Crown Publishing Group
A division of Penguin Random House LLC
1745 Broadway
New York, NY 10019
tenspeed.com
penguinrandomhouse.com

Typefaces: Asenbayu's Broone, Luzi Type's Messina Serif, and Luzi Type's Messina Sans

Library of Congress Cataloging-in-Publication Data
Names: German, Nelson, 1981– author | Gray, Andréa Lawson, 1954– author | Gonzalez, Eduardo (Photographer) photographer | Fabre, Fanesha illustrator
Title: Caribbean cocktails : drinks and bites from the Afro-Latino diaspora / by Nelson German with Andréa Lawson Gray ; photographs by Eduardo Gonzalez ; illustrations by Fanesha Fabre.
Identifiers: LCCN 2025025688 (print) | LCCN 2025025689 (ebook) | ISBN 9780593837740 Hardcover | ISBN 9780593837757 Ebook
Subjects: LCSH: Cocktails | Cooking, Dominican | African diaspora—History | Black people—Caribbean area | Latin Americans—Caribbean area | LCGFT: Cookbooks
Classification: LCC TX951 .G4355 2026 (print) | LCC TX951 (ebook) | DDC 641.87/4097293—dc23/eng/20250702
LC record available at https://lccn.loc.gov/2025025688
LC ebook record available at https://lccn.loc.gov/2025025689

Hardcover ISBN 978-0-593-83774-0
Ebook ISBN 978-0-593-83775-7

Editor: Claire Yee | Production editor: Terry Deal
Designer: Betsy Stromberg | Production designer: Mari Gill
Production manager: Jane Chinn | Prepress color manager: Claudia Sanchez
Prop stylist: Andréa Lawson Gray | Photo assistant: Danielle Gonzalez
Copy editor: Allie Kiekhofer | Proofreaders: Patricia Dailey, Lydia O'Brien
Indexer: Heather Laskey
Publicist: Natalie Yera-Campbell | Marketer: Joey Lozada

Art on page 25: © Shutterstock.com/lukpedclub.

Manufactured in China

10 9 8 7 6 5 4 3 2 1

First Edition

The authorized representative in the EU for product safety and compliance is Penguin Random House Ireland, Morrison Chambers, 32 Nassau Street, Dublin D02 YH68, Ireland, https://eu-contact.penguin.ie.

"There are chefs who cook food and craft drinks that look good, and then there are chefs like German, who craft consumable creations that feel good. The kind that make you pause mid-sip and think, *Wait, how did he do that?* and then, a second later, *Why does this taste like home?*

Nelson doesn't just craft recipes, he tells stories through ingredients, memories, and that quiet kind of confidence that comes from knowing exactly who you are. He cooks like he lives, with generosity and soul. *Caribbean Cocktails* captures that completely."

—**AVISHAR BARUA**, chef and founder of Agni, Joya's, and Seriously Fun Hospitality

"German's stunning new book showcases the vibrant flavors of the Afro-Latino diaspora. *Caribbean Cocktails* brings forth a collection of recipes that not only celebrates the rich culinary heritage of the Caribbean but also shows that comforting flavors rooted in tradition are simple enough to come alive in your own home bar and kitchen."

—**ILLYANNA MAISONET**, James Beard Award–winning author of *Diasporican: A Puerto Rican Cookbook*